JUNIOR COLLEGE DISTRICT
of St. Louis - St. Louis County
LIBRARY
7508 Forsyth Blvd.
St. Louis, Missouri 63105

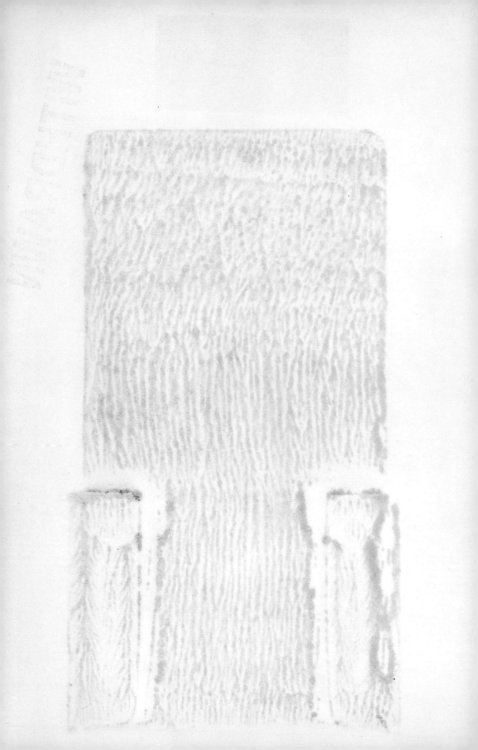

THE ODES OF PINDAR

THE ODES

OF PINDAR

TRANSLATED BY
RICHMOND LATTIMORE

PHOENIX BOOKS

THE UNIVERSITY OF CHICAGO PRESS

CHICAGO & LONDON

A NOTE ON PINDAR AND HIS POETRY

CONCERNING the life of Pindar we can be sure only of the bare outlines, together with certain general facts. There is no sound biographical tradition for his period. It will perhaps be best to ignore anecdotes, guesses, and combinations which cannot be confirmed and to state briefly what seems to be established. Pindar was born a citizen of Thebes, the chief city of the Boiotian confederacy, in 518 B.C. The date of his death is uncertain; but the last work of his for which we have a date (though not a very secure one) is the Eighth Pythian, written probably in 446 B.C. At all events, he lived to an advanced age. We know further that he was of aristocratic birth and heir to certain priestly offices of the sort highly prized by the Greek nobility. In spite of his high rank, he plainly did not consider himself wealthy; but the simple list of his contracts indicates that he was a professional poet of great repute, and as such he must have earned a great deal. The rest of his biography must be pieced out from the contents and implications of his poems, many of which are dated.

Pindar lived through a period of crucial change in Greek history. His life is bisected by the great Persian invasion of 480–479 B.C., a war in which Thebes, split within by factional rivalries, played a difficult and unhappy part. Against the forces of Xerxes, the combined Greek command chose to defend central Greece by holding the mountain pass of Thermopylai and the sea pass of Artemision. The Persians forced them to give up both positions. Theban soldiers had fought beside Leonidas at Thermopylai—badly, according to Herodotos, but he is prejudiced and may be wrong. In any case, when the Greek armies fell back on the Isthmos of Korinth and the fleet on Salamis, Boiotia and all other states to the north were left open to the enemy; nor had the Thebans the opportunity, as did the Athenians, to evacuate their population by sea. Thebes gave in, the city was in the hands of the Persians and Persian sympathizers, and the Persian general, Mardonios, made it his base of operations. At Plataia, where the invaders were finally defeated and forced to withdraw, a Theban contingent fought on the Persian side. What part, if any, Pindar played in all this is not known; but for some years after Plataia he was a citizen of a dishonored state. Parallels from modern wars are only too obvious, and it should be understandable that a certain bitterness over this defeat and betrayal and over the attitude of more fortunate states with better war records remained with Pindar. Of the cities which fought the Persian, Athens in particular emerged from the struggle with greatly augmented prestige and strength. Pindar is said to have studied at Athens and undoubtedly had many friends there; but his openly avowed admiration for Athenian achievement must have been tempered with resentment even before, in or about 457 B.C., the Athenians temporarily forced Thebes into the position of a subordinate ally.

As a professional poet, Pindar traveled much, and his acquaintance was singularly wide. His poems (including the fragments) show connections in all the leading Greek states of his day and with many small cities as well. Among these external relations there are several which are of particular importance. He wrote several poems in honor of Hieron, tyrant (that is, dictator) of Syracuse in Sicily, and considered that cruel, but gifted and successful, ruler to be his friend. In Greek history aristocrats are seldom found on the side of tyrants; but Pindar thought he saw in Hieron a champion of Greek civilization against the dark forces of barbarism (*Pyth.* 1) and a ruler intelligent enough to use his vast power toward ultimate good. Pindar himself visited Sicily, and his works show acquaintance with other prominent Sicilians, including Theron, tyrant of Akragas, and, in particular, Theron's nephew, Thrasyboulos.

Another important external connection is Pindar's friendship with various noble families in Aigina, a Dorian island-state across the water from Athens. The friendship between Thebes and Aigina was close, and in legend the nymphs Thebe and Aigina were said to be sisters. Pindar wrote eleven odes for Aiginetan victors—almost one-fourth of the total number—and did not weary of singing the praises of their special heroes, the Aiakidai, or sons of Aiakos, namely, Peleus and Telamon, with their sons, Achilleus and Aias (Ajax). The Aiginetans, famous seafarers who distinguished themselves at Salamis, were also victims of Athenian imperialism (their state was "liquidated" by Athens during the Peloponnesian War), and it is tempting to see in *Pythia* 8 a protest against the pretensions of the Athenian democracy led by Perikles. Yet, if this is true, too many conclusions concerning Pindar's political views should not be recklessly drawn. Despite certain aristocratic prejudices, he belonged (apparently) to no faction; when he speaks of states, he generally speaks only to praise; and he considers himself to be in sympathy with all intelligent and well-meaning men, whatever their city (*Pyth.* 1, 2, 11).

Of Pindar's works, only the epinician, or victory, odes have survived intact, although numerous fragments show that he wrote much besides. The victory ode commemorates the success of a winner in the "games" or athletic meets held at regular intervals from very early times down to the Roman period. There were four great games: the Olympian, at Pisa in Elis, sacred to Zeus; the Pythian, at Pytho (Delphoi), sacred to Apollo; the Nemean, at Nemea in the Peloponnese, sacred to Zeus; and the Isthmian, at the Isthmos of Korinth, sacred to Poseidon. Of these, the Olympian games were the oldest and most honorable. In addition, there were numerous local games, in which success brought minor, but considerable, acclaim; many of these are named in poems for famous champions, such as Diagoras of Rhodes (*Ol.* 7) or Xenophon of Korinth (*Ol.* 13). The events included races for four-horse chariot, mule chariot, and single (ridden) horse; foot races at various distances; contests in boxing, wrestling, and pankration (a combination of the two); and the pentathlon, a complex event which involved racing, jumping, throwing the discus and javelin, and wrestling. It must be understood that in all horse and chariot races the "victor" was the person who entered horse or team; he was not required to ride or drive in person.

Pindar's peculiar excellence seems to have lain in the composition of victory odes; they may well have been his favorite form. The modern reader will always wonder why. There are several considerations. In the first place, the games were occasions of high sanctity, held in holy places, and protected by a truce of God, invoked to secure free competition; it will be seen that every epinician ode wears, in one place or another, the attributes of a hymn. Further, success meant a demonstration of wealth and power (particularly in the chariot races) or of superb physical prowess, shown through peaceful and harmless means. The very uselessness of these triumphs, which aroused the contemptuous anger of Xenophanes and Euripides, attracted Pindar. A victory meant that time, expense, and hard work had been lavished on an achievement which brought no calculable advantage, only honor and beauty. This may sound somewhat romantic, but competition symbolized an idea of nobility which meant much to Pindar; and in the exaltation of victory he seems sometimes to see a kind of transfiguration, briefly making radiant a world which most of the time seemed, to him as to his contemporaries, dark and brutal.

The occasion and circumstances of the ode must have been somewhat as follows: When a victory was won, the victor (or his family or some wealthy friend) commissioned the poet to write the commemorative ode. When this was complete, a choir of men or boys (probably amateurs and friends of the victor) was trained to sing it. The true presentation of the ode was, then, a performance, privately given for the victor and his friends sometime after the event. Pindar himself was not always present at the performance, nor did he always train the choir. In commissioning, some sort of agreement or contract was made. This contract may often have concerned not only the poet's fee but also various matters which the person who paid for the ode desired to have included, such as, for instance, mythical allusions to be made or details concerning the victor or his family. Thus, when we find Pindar being rather tediously exact about the exploits of brothers, uncles, cousins, or remote ancestors of his hero, we must remember that all this may have been stipulated in the contract. At other times he was doubtless given a free hand.

Concerning the form of the ode, there has been much discussion. This is not the place for me to set forth a thesis or to defend one in detail; I shall simply state what I take to be the general principles of composition. The poet had before him certain matters which must be included; the name of the victor, the place of the victory with some allusion to the protective deity of the place, one or more stories or episodes from heroic legend (in all but very short odes), and any further elaboration which was called for in the contract or which suggested itself to the poet. Above all, it was necessary to make a beginning. Pindar's opening passages are generally imposing, elaborate, and worked out with great care (note, by contrast, that *terminal* passages may be abrupt, even awkward). He may begin with an invocation addressed to a god or city (*Ol.* 4, 12, 14; *Pyth.* 1, 2, 8; etc.); with a comparison or simile (*Ol.* 6, 7; Isth. 6); with a wish (*Pyth.* 3); with a direct address to the victor (*Isth.* 2) or a statement of the poet's own position and obligations (*Ol.* 3, 10; *Pyth.* 4); or with various combinations of the above motives (*Ol.* 1; *Nem.* 5; etc.). From such a formal opening he proceeds by way of compliment and acknowledgment to the rest of his

ix

material. The manner is that of an improvisation, so that (for example) a myth is generally introduced as if it were not planned or foreseen but suggested out of the immediate context. How much of this forward development represents actual method, how much means only a contrived appearance of improvisation, it is difficult to say.

Since it is necessary to speak of the victor at the beginning, either in or immediately after the invocation, and since it is natural also to end with the victor or with persons close to him, the natural place for the myth or episode out of heroic legend—that part of the material most remote from the present—is in the center. But here, as always, there is no hard and fast rule. In *Nemea* 1 and 10 the myth runs from the middle of the poem right to the close. Again, in *Pythia* 1 (as also elsewhere) there is no one myth, but various mythical descriptions and allusions are scattered throughout the ode.

Nothing could be more deceptive than to emphasize too much the parts of the poem (invocation, personal compliment, prayer, moral, myth) as sharply distinct elements which must be bound together by transitional ties. It is better to admit that the transitional passages, such as moralities, wishes, comparisons, may grow directly out of what precedes and may generate what follows. Consider, first, for example, the beginning of *Pythia* 10 (the earliest ode). Pindar's opening note is the happiness of Thessaly (and of Lakedaimon, a foil to show *how* happy Thessaly is). After brief self-adjuration, he gathers up the elements of the victory (in naming the winner, his home, the place of the contest); then proceeds, via the victory of Hippokleas' father and Apollo's favor, to prayer that such successes may continue unbroken and the gods' favor be constant. Yet no mortal can always be happy, though the success of father and son after him symbolizes such fortune as can be attained by men, beyond whose reach lies the divine happiness of the Hyperboreans. Through these moralities thought is swung against counterthought until the illustrative name, Hyperboreans, chimes the keynote of the myth, which follows. Here invocation, occasion, victor, prayer, moral, and myth are more or less discernible elements, though the development is so smooth that we pass naturally, even unconsciously, from one stage to another (here, as often, the return from myth to occasion and victor is less happily accomplished). Contrast, now, *Pythia* 8 (the latest ode). This opens with invocation of Hesychia, the goddess of peace, who is besought to accept the song in honor of Aristomenes, the victor. But peace and justice evoke, by way of contrast, hatred and pride, as embodied in the giants Porphyrion and Typhon. Their fall came about at the hands of Zeus and Apollo; and Apollo, lord of Pytho, brings us once more to the victory, the victor, and Aigina. Invocation, victor, myth, moral, and warning are inextricably intertwined. This is no fusion of parts but an organic development from the idea of Hesychia and the presence of Aristomenes; and the rest of the poem can be run through in the same manner.

At the same time, there are many mythical passages which were doubtless forecast in advance and which are to some extent self-subsistent entities. The best example is the story of Jason in *Pythia* 4, which opens formally and closes not through overlapping phrase but through an abrupt, conscious summary and an equally formal and conscious return to the victor, Arkesilas. Even in such "pure myths," Pindar hardly tells a story, for he assumed that the outlines of legend were familiar to his listeners; rather, he lights up some intense moment, or series of moments, in a tale already known.

Further, although embarrassment over the terms of hire and the status of the poet as paid entertainer breaks to the surface, Pindar likes to appear as one who writes as he pleases, being the friend and equal of his patrons. These allowed the great man much liberty. Thus he feels free to moralize as he will, even in the middle of a myth (*Ol.* 1); to correct himself in mid-progress (*Ol.* 1, 8); to talk to himself (*Pyth.* 2); to defend his own position and policies (*Pyth.* 9,

11; *Nem.* 7, 8); to make entirely personal acknowledgments (*Pyth.* 8). And here, perhaps, is one more reason for Pindar's devotion to the epinician ode; it gave him a starting-point, from which he could evolve, within certain limits, almost any sort of variation on the choral ode and, at the same time, a firm point of reference to which he could always return.

Pindar's odes are generally cast in triads, each triad consisting of two identical stanzas, called "strophe" and "antistrophe," followed by a third which is different, called "epode." In any given poem, all triads are identical. In a few of the odes there are no triads, but a series of identical stanzas (*Ol.* 14; *Pyth.* 6, 12; *Nem.* 2, 4, 9; *Isth.* 8). Such odes are called "monostrophic." The meters are exceedingly complex; but, though scholars are unable to agree with one another over definitions, they are able to gain a very definite idea of the rhythms involved.

The obscurity commonly attributed to Pindar is mainly due to his allusiveness, that is, his habit of plunging obliquely into legendary matter or personal compliment where we have lost the clues. Also, to any but an experienced classicist (and sometimes to one of these) his work will seem at times to be formidably studded with proper names. These cannot be excised, and the translator can only furnish a glossary and hope that his readers will be patient enough to use it if they need to. Another inherent source of difficulty is stylistic. Sentences are long, main verbs often hang fire, shifts of subject or emphasis may be sudden. Even so, Pindar is never quite so desperately difficult as Browning (*Sordello*), Keats ("Lamia"), or Shelley ("Prometheus Unbound") can be; but where the new reader finds that he cannot make sense, he may feel sure that he is dealing with a passage which has perplexed scholars and probably (I am thinking of Sogenes, of *Nem.* 7) the poet's own listeners. At his dazzling best, Pindar is perfectly clear; I can only hope that this will come out in the translation.

OLYMPIA 1

Best of all things is water; but gold, like a gleaming fire
by night, outshines all pride of wealth beside.
But, my heart, would you chant the glory of games,
look never beyond the sun
by day for any star shining brighter through the deserted air,
nor any contest than Olympia greater to sing.
It is thence that the song winds strands
in the hearts of the skilled to celebrate
the son of Kronos. They come their ways
to the magnificent board of Hieron,

who handles the scepter of dooms in Sicily, rich in flocks,
reaping the crested heads of every excellence.
There his fame is magnified
in the splendor of music, where
we delight at the friendly table. Then take the Dorian lyre
   from its peg,
if any glory of Pisa or Pherenikos
slide with delight beneath your heart,
when by Alpheus waters he sped
his bulk, with the lash laid never on,
and mixed in the arms of victory his lord,

king of Syracuse, delighting in horses; and his fame shines
among strong men where Lydian Pelops went to dwell,
Pelops that he who clips the earth in his great strength,
Poseidon, loved when Klotho lifted him out
of the clean cauldron, his shoulder gleaming ivory.
Great marvels in truth are these, but tales
told and overlaid with elaboration of lies
amaze men's wits against the true word.

1

Grace, who brings to fulfilment all things for men's delight,
granting honor again, many a time makes
things incredible seem true.
Days to come are the wisest witnesses.
It is better for a man to speak well of the gods; he is less to
  blame.
Son of Tantalos, against older men I will say
that when your father summoned the gods
to that stateliest feast at beloved Sipylos,
and gave them to eat and received in turn,
then he of the shining trident caught you up,

his heart to desire broken, and with his horses and car of gold
carried you up to the house of Zeus and his wide honor,
where Ganymede at a later time
came for the same desire in Zeus.
But when you were gone, and men from your mother looked,
  nor brought you back,
some man, a neighbor, spoke quietly for spite,
how they took you and with a knife
minced your limbs into bubbling water
and over the table divided and ate
flesh of your body, even to the last morsel.

I cannot understand how a god could gorge thus; I recoil.
Many a time disaster has come to the speakers of evil.
If they who watch on Olympos have honored
any man, that man was Tantalos; but he was not
able to swallow his great fortune, and for his high stomach
drew a surpassing doom when our father
hung the weight of the stone above him.
He waits ever the stroke at his head and is divided from joy.

That life is too much for his strength; he is buckled fast in
  torment,
agony fourth among three others, because he stole

2

and gave to his own fellowship
that ambrosia and nectar
wherewith the gods made him immortal. If any man thinks
   to swindle
God, he is wrong. Therefore, they sent his son
back to the fleeting destiny of man's race.
And when at the time of life's blossoming
the first beard came to darken his cheek,
he thought on winning a bride ready at hand,

Hippodameia, the glorious daughter of a king in Pisa.
He walked alone in the darkness by the gray sea,
invoking the lord of the heavy trident,
and he appeared clear at his feet.
He spoke: "Look you, Poseidon, if you have had any joy
   of my love
and the Kyprian's sweet gifts, block the brazen spear
of Oinomaos, and give me the fleeter chariot
by Elis' river, and clothe me about in strength.
Thirteen suitors he has killed now, and ever
puts aside the marriage of his daughter.

The great danger never descends upon a man without
   strength;
but if we are destined to die, why should one sit
to no purpose in darkness and find a nameless old age
without any part of glory his own? So my way
lies this hazard; yours to accomplish the end."
He spoke, with words not wide of the mark.
The god, increasing his fame, gave him
a golden chariot and horses never weary with wings.

Breaking the strength of Oinomaos, he took the maiden and
   brought her to bed.
She bore him six sons, lords of the people, blazing in valor.
Now he lies at the Alpheos
crossing, mixed with the mighty dead.

3

His tomb is thronged about at the altar where many strangers
    pass; but the glory
of Pelops looks afar from Olympia
in the courses where speed is matched with speed
and a man's force harsh at the height.
And the winner the rest of his lifetime
keeps happiness beside him sweeter than honey

as far as the games go; but the good that stays by day and
    abides with him
is best that can come to a man. Be it my work to crown
in the rider's rhythm and strain
of Aiolis that king. I believe
there is no man greater both ways, for wisdom in beautiful
    things and power's weight
we shall ever glorify by skill in the folds of song.
Some god stands ever about you, musing
in his mind over what you do,
Hieron. May he not leave you soon.
So shall I hope to find once more

even a sweeter word's way to sing and help the chariot
    fleeting,
coming again to the lifting hill of Kronos. For me
the Muse in her might is forging yet the strongest arrow.
One man is excellent one way, one in another; the highest
fulfils itself in kings. Oh, look no further.
Let it be yours to walk this time on the height.
Let it be mine to stand beside you
in victory, for my skill at the forefront of the Hellenes.

OLYMPIA 2

My songs, lords of the lyre,
which of the gods, what hero, what mortal shall we celebrate?
Zeus has Pisa; but Herakles founded the Olympiad
out of spoils of his warfare;
but Theron, for his victory with chariot-four, is the man
we must sing now, him of the kind regard to strangers,
the tower Akragantine,
choice bud of a high line guarding the city.

In strong toil of the spirit
they were the eye of Sicily, they beside the river kept
the sacred house; their doom drew on, bringing wealth and
    delight near
by the valor in their blood.
But, O Kronios, Rhea's son, guarding Olympos' throne
and the games' glory and the Alpheos crossing,
in mild mood for the song's sake
kind keep for them always the land of their fathers

the rest of their generation. Of things come to pass
in justice or unjust, not Time the father
of all can make the end unaccomplished.
But forgetfulness may come still with happiness.
Grief, breaking again out of quiet, dies at last, quenched
under the waxing weight of fair things,

with God's destiny dropping
wealth deep from above. Thus the tale for the queenly
daughters of Kadmos, who endured much; grief falls a dead
    weight
as goods wax in strength. Semele

of the delicate hair, who died in the thunderstroke,
lives on Olympos, beloved of Pallas forever, of Zeus,
best loved of her son with ivy in his hands.

And they say that in the sea
among the daughters of Nereus in the depth, Ino
is given life imperishable for all time. But for mortal men
no limit in death has been set apart
when we shall bring to an end in unbroken good
the sun's child, our day of quiet; stream upon stream
of delights mixed with labor descends upon men.

Thus Destiny, who has from her father
the kindly guidance of these men, yet with wealth sent from
    God
bestows some pain also, to return upon us hereafter.
So his doomed son killed Laios
when they met, and brought to accomplishment
the thing foretold long since at Pytho.

And Erinys looked on him in bitterness
and slew all his strong race at each others' hands.
Yet when Polyneikes fell, Thersandros remained for honor
in the trial of fresh battles,
a branch to shield the house of Adrastos.
Stemmed in his stock, it is fit for Ainesidamos' son
to win songs in his honor and the lyre's sound.

He himself took the prize
at Olympia; to his brother equal in right the impartial
Graces brought blossoms of honor for the twelve-lap chariot
    race
at Pytho, at the Isthmos; success
for the striver washes away the effort of striving.
Wealth elaborate with virtue brings opportunity for various
deeds; it shoulders the cruel depth of care,

star-bright, man's truest
radiance; if a man keep it and know the future,
how, as we die here, the heart uncontrolled
yields retribution; likewise for sins in this kingdom of God
there is a judge under the earth. He gives sentence
in constraint of wrath.

But with nights equal forever,
with sun equal in their days, the good men
have life without labor, disquieting not the earth in strength
   of hand,
never the sea's water
for emptiness of living. Beside the high gods
they who had joy in keeping faith lead a life
without tears. The rest look on a blank face of evil.

But they who endure thrice over
in the world beyond to keep their souls from all sin
have gone God's way to the tower of Kronos; there
winds sweep from the Ocean
across the Island of the Blessed. Gold flowers to flame
on land in the glory of trees; it is fed in the water,
whence they bind bracelets to their arms and go chapleted

under the straight decrees of Rhadamanthys,
whom the husband of Rhea, high throned above all,
our great father, keeps in the chair of state beside him.
They say Peleus is there, and Kadmos,
and his mother with prayer softening Zeus' heart
carried Achilles thither,

who felled Hektor, Troy's unassailable
tall column of strength, who gave death to Kyknos
and the Aithiop, Dawn's child. There are many sharp shafts
   in the quiver
under the crook of my arm.

7

They speak to the understanding; most men need inter-
  preters.
The wise man knows many things in his blood; the vulgar
  are taught.
They will say anything. They clatter vainly like crows

against the sacred bird of Zeus.
Come, my heart, strain the bow to the mark now. Whom
  shall we strike
in gentleness, slipping merciful arrows? Toward Akragas
we will bend the bow and speak
a word under oath in sincerity of mind.
Not in a hundred years has a city given forth
a man kinder to his friends, more open of hand

than Theron. But envy bestrides praise,
though coupled not with justice; still the revilers'
scandal would put secrecy upon fair deeds
of noble men. For sands escape number,
and of all the joy Theron has brought to others
what man could tell the measure?

My claim is to sing bright Akragas and please the Tyndari-
  dai, the lovers of strangers,
and their sister Helen with the splendid hair,
shaping the hymn of Olympic triumph for Theron, the speed
  of his horses
with feet never weary. So the Muse was near as I found a
  fire-new style
to set in the Dorian cast the speech

of acclamation. The wreaths bound over my hair are an
  influence
to this duty formed in the hands of God,
to mix the lyre's intricate voice, the clamor of flutes, and the
  set of the words
for Ainesidamos' son the right way; and Pisa bids me speak.
  From her,
driven of God, songs speed to a man,

over whose locks and brows an upright judge of the Hellenes,
an Aitolian, fulfilling the ordinances of Herakles
anciently founded, has cast
the pale glory of the olive that long ago,
from the shadowy springs of Ister,
Amphitryon's son brought back, to be
the loveliest memorial of the games at Olympia.

By reason he persuaded the Hyperboreans, Apollo's people.
In sincerity of heart he asked, for the grove of Zeus
open to all, that growth to shadow men always and crown
  their valor.

Before this in his time, when his father's altars were hallowed, at mid-month,
it had cast back the full orb of evening,

riding in gold. He established the sacred test of the fifth-year games
under the magic hanging hills of Alpheus river.
But the lawn in the valley of Kronian Pelops had blossomed not to the beauty of trees.
He thought the garden, naked of these, must endure the sun's sharp rays.
Then it was the urge took him to journey

to Istrian country. There Leto's daughter, the runner with horses,
received him when he came from Arkadia's ridges and winding gullies,
when, at Eurystheus' command,
the doom of his father had driven him
to bring the doe with the golden horns
that once Taygeta had written in fee
to be sacred to Artemis Orthosia.

On that errand he saw the land at the back of the cold north wind,
and he stood amazed at the trees.
A sweet longing came upon him to plant them at the twelve-lap running place
of horses. Now he visits in graciousness that festival, with the godlike
twins, the children of deep-girdled Leda.

He came to Olympos and left those heroes guidance of the magnificent games,
man's might and the chariot's speed handled.

I will speak, for my heart drives me: on the children of
    Emmenos
and Theron glory is descended at the hands of the Tyndari-
    dai, since beyond others
they propitiate them at the bountiful feasting-table,

keeping in reverence of heart the gods' mysteries.
But if water is best of all things, and of possessions gold is
    goodliest,
still in the virtues of men
Theron has come home to the uttermost
Herakles' pillars
and touched. Beyond no wise man can tread;
no fool either. I will not venture; a fool were I.

Mightiest driver of the weariless speed in the lightning's feet,
Zeus: the circling seasons, yours,
have brought me to testify
to the wide strength of highest achievements
by virtue of song and the lyre's intricacy.
At friends' good luck the noble will rise to welcome
the sweet message.
O son of Kronos, lord of Aitna,
blast-furnace to hundred-headed Typhon's bulk,
in the name of the Graces
accept this song of Olympic victory,

light at long last from the wide strength of valor.
For it rides the wheels of Psaumis,
who, his brow shaded in olive
of Pisa, comes home, bringing glory
on Kamarina. May God be kindly
to his prayers hereafter; I have praise for him.
A keen handler of horses,
he rejoices in hospitality to his friends;
and his face, with clean purpose, is turned toward Peace, who
    loves cities.
I will not steep my speech
in lies; the test of any man lies in action.

So the son of Klymenos
was set free of dishonor
at the hands of Lemnian women.
As he won the race in bronze armor
and came to Hypsipyle for his garland, he spoke:
"Here am I in my speed.
My hands are as good as my heart.
Many a time even on young men gray hairs
appear, against the likelihood of their youth."

OLYMPIA 5

Accept, daughter of Ocean, in kindness of heart the blos-
soming
to delight of high deeds and Olympian garlands
for the mule car and the tireless feet, accept these gifts from
Psaumis.

Increasing your city, Kamarina, that fosters its people,
he honored six double altars at the high festivals of the gods
with the sacrifice of oxen and with five-day games, races

for team, mules, single horse. A winner, to you
he dedicated the delicate glory
and proclaimed his father Akron and the new-established
dwelling.

He comes from the lovely precinct of Oinomaos and Pelops
and lifts again, Pallas, keeper of the city, your sacred wood,
your river Oanis with the lake near by,

and the stately channels whereby Hipparis waters the folk.
With speed he welds the high-groined forest of standing
houses,
bringing back out of despair to the light this people, his
citizens.

Always attendant on valor, work and substance struggle to
win
the end veiled in danger;
but when men succeed, even their neighbors think them
wise.

13

Savior Zeus, high in the clouds, at home on the Kronian hill,
with honor for the wide course of Alpheos and the sacred
   cave of Ida,
I come to you a suppliant, speaking above Lydian flutes.

I will ask that you glorify this city with fame
of good men; and you, Olympic champion, may you carry
your age in happiness to its end, with joy in Poseidon's horses,

your sons standing beside you, Psaumis. But if one water
   flowering wealth
in abundance of substance
and fair fame also, let him not seek to become God.

OLYMPIA 6

Like architects of a sumptuous palace,
who set the golden columns under the portico wall,
we shall build. The forehead of every work
begun must shine from afar. If a man be Olympian victor,
steward at the mantic altar of Zeus in Pisa,
cofounder of glorious Syracuse, what praise shall he escape
in the song's loveliness, given only citizens without rancor?

Let the son of Sostratos know
in that cast he has set his blessed feet. Accomplishments
without venture win no praise among men
nor in hollow ships; splendor of toil is remembered of many.
Agesias, beside you stands that praise that of old
in justice Adrastos spoke of Amphiaraos,
the seer Oikleidas, when earth folded him under and his
    shining horses.

Seven corpse-fires burned to the end, and Talaos' son
spoke at Thebes this word: "I mourn the glory of the host.
He was two things, a good prophet, a fighter with the pike."
    Such praise
befalls the lord of the feast at Syracuse.
I, who am not bitter in disputation nor overbold,
owe plain testimony and swear a great oath
over the words; and the sweet-voiced Muses shall hear me
    speak.

Up then, Phintis, yoke me the strength of the mules
with speed, let me mount the chariot, drive a clean
highway to the source of these men's race.
They understand, and will guide us better than others;
they took garlands at Olympia. Now before them

we must open the gates of song; to Pitana
and the bank of Eurotas we must take our journey today.

Pitana, the legends tell, lay in love with Poseidon, Kronos'
   son,
and bore the dark-haired girl, Euadne. She hid
under the fold of her robe her maiden love's agony,
till in the final month she sent attendants to carry
the child, and give it into the hands of Eilatidas,
lord of the men of Arkady at Phaisana, with Alpheos under
   his sway.
There grown, by Apollo she first touched Aphrodite's sweet-
   ness.

But Aipytos knew the whole time how she hid the seed of
   the god.
To Pytho, with sharp care crushing down the wrath in his
   heart unspoken,
he departed, to question the god over grief unendurable;
while she, putting aside her girdle, crimson dyed,
and her silver pitcher, under the darkness of low trees
bore a boy with the heart of divination. The gold-haired god
made gentle Eleithuia and the Destinies to stand beside her.

Out of the lovely distress at her loins came Iamos
straightway into the light, whom she in her grief
left on the ground. By the god's design two
green-eyed serpents tended him, with blameless venom dis-
   tilled
of bees. The king, riding from rocky Pytho,
questioned all in the house when he came for the child
Euadne had borne, and called him issue

of Phoibos, to be beyond all men a seer among mortals
pre-eminent, nor his race fail ever thereafter.
Thus Aipytos. They swore they had heard
never nor seen the five-day child. He lay

16

in the long grass and a wilderness of thicket, his soft body
deep over in the blue and yellow brightness of violets,
whereby his mother declared upon him for all time

that name immortal, Iamos. He, assuming in time the bloom
of delightful youth, gold-chapleted, wading in Alpheos mid-
   stream, called
his forefather strong Poseidon, and the archer over god-built
   Delos
under the night sky, claiming upon his head
the care of subjects. Close to his ear his father's voice came
answering, and spoke: "Arise my son, follow
here in the wake of my voice to the place frequented of all."

They came to the sheer rock of towering Kronios.
There the god gave into his hands a double treasure:
seercraft, to hear even then the voice ignorant
of lies: and command—when the bold contriver should
   come,
Herakles, proud blossom of Alkaid blood, and found
in his father's name the festival thronged of men, prime
   ordinance of contests—
to establish on Zeus' highest altar the place of prophecy.

From him, the Iamid race with their high fame in Hellas.
Wealth came afterward; they honor accomplishment;
the way they walk is clear, and each thing
bears witness. Mockery from malice of others overhangs
their heads who drive foremost over the twelve-lap course,
with grave grace pouring glorification of comeliness on
   them.
But if in truth under Kyllana's peaks, Agesias, your mother's
   kinsmen

propitiate over and again the gods' herald with supplication
of sacrifice in piety, Hermes, who keeps the games and the
   luck of the contest

to magnify the good men of Arkadia, he, son of Sostratos,
abets the weight of his father's thunder to grant you fortune.
I believe a stone upon my speech has honed it to fluency,
and the mother of my mothers, the Stymphalian, blossoming
    Metope,
urges my will compliant with the easy breath of persuasion.

Her child is Thebe, bender of horses, whose lovely waters
I drink, and the men I braid this complication of song for are
comrades in arms. Up with your men, Aineas!
Sing first Hera of maidenhood, then know
if in true account we escape the ancient
word of shame, swine of Boiotia. You are a true messenger,
letterstaff of the comely-haired Muses, sweet mixing-bowl of
    vociferous song.

I have told you to remember Syracuse and Ortygia.
Hieron in serious thought controls them under
his scepter's candid sweep; he guides the crimson feet
of the feast of Demeter and the lady of white horses, her
    daughter,
with the power of Zeus on Aitna. The soft-spoken lyres
acknowledge him, and the dancing. May lurking time not
    shatter his power.
Let him receive in kindly affection Agesias' victor feast,

sped from home at the keep of Stymphalos to his second
    home,
leaving the mother-city of Arkady rich in sheep. In the night
    of storms
it is well to have two anchors binding the fleet ship.
May God's love appoint the glory of both my friends.
Lord of the sea's action, consort of Amphitrite,
her of the golden spindle, grant a straight voyage, clear
of distress. Make blossom the joyous flower of my song.

18

OLYMPIA 7

As one who takes a cup from a lavish hand,
bubbling within the foam of the grape,
presenting it
to a young bridegroom, pledging hearth to hearth, the pride,
    sheer gold, of possession,
the joy of the feast, to honor his new son, render him
among friends present admired for the bride's consent:

so I, bringing poured nectar of victory,
gift of the Muses, the mind's sweet yield,
offer it up
to the conquerors at Olympia and Pytho. Blessed is he whom
    good fame surrounds.
Grace eyes one man, then another, bestowing favor
frequently to the melodious lyre and the manifold music of
    flutes;

and to both strains I keep company with Diagoras, singing
the sea's child, daughter of Aphrodite and bride of Helios,
    Rhodes,
and give praise, spoil of his boxing, to the onslaught of a
    man gigantic,
wreathed in victory beside Alpheos' water
and Kastalia; and to Damagetos his father, darling of Justice,
who dwell in the triple-citied island over against
the jut of broad Asia, by right of an Argive spear.

I will try to straighten the story from the beginning
with news from as far back as Tlepolemos
for Herakles'
race of reaching strength. On the father's side they glory in
    Zeus' descent; on the mother's,

19

Amyntoridai from Astydameia. Delusions innumerable
hang their shadows over men's minds. This thing passes wit
  to discover,

what is best now and at the end for a man to attain.
Even Tlepolemos, this island's founder, once
angered, rearing
the stock of brute olive, smote to death Alkmana's bastard
  brother,
Likymnios, at Tiryns as he issued from the chamber of Midea.
  Despair in the brain has driven
even the wise man out of his course. He went to the god for
  counsel.

From the fragrant sanctuary the gold-haired god bespoke a
  voyage
of ships from the Lernaian ness straight for a seagirt reach,
where once the high king of the gods drenched their city in
  a gold snowfall,
when, by the artifice of Hephaistos,
at the stroke of the bronze-heeled axe Athene sprang
from the height of her father's head with a strong cry.
The sky shivered before her and earth our mother.

Then Hyperion's giant son, light-giver to mortals,
laid a necessity upon his own children
to guard thereafter:
they must be first to found a bright altar to the goddess and
  establish a stately sacrifice
and propitiate the heart of her father and the maid of the
  ringing spear. Respect
for forethought puts on men goodliness and delight also.

Yet the unpredictable mist of forgetfulness stalks us,
it wrenches aside the right way of action
far from our thoughts.

Thus they went up, having not the bright seed of flame, with
    fireless sacrament they appointed
the grove on the acropolis. Yet he, assembling the yellow
    cloud,
rained much gold upon them, and the green-eyed goddess
    granted

every art, that they should surpass all men in the excellent
    work of their hands.
And their streets grew images in the likeness of men and
    beasts.
Their fame went deep. For the wise skill will wax greater
    for its innocence.
The ancient legends of men
tell how, when Zeus and the immortals divided the earth
Rhodes had not yet shone in the sea's water,
but the island was hidden in the salt depths.

Helios was gone, and none showed forth his lot.
They left him with no guerdon of land,
that blameless god.
He spoke, and Zeus would cast again, but Helios would not
    suffer it, for he said
under the gray sea he had spied, as a growth from the floor,
a land to foster multitudes, kindly to sheep.

Straightway he bade Lachesis of the golden veil
lift up her hands, nor deny
the gods' great oath
but assent with the son of Kronos, bending her head; the
    island rising thereafter
into the bright air should be his. The words' end was ac-
    complished
with a true fall. Out of the winding water the island

blossomed, held of the father of searing sun-rays,
master of horses that breathe fire. Rhodes mixed with him
    bore

seven sons, that displayed the shrewdest wits of the men of
old time.
Of these, one sired Kamiros,
Ialysos, eldest born, and Lindos; sundered, they held
the land of their patrimony in triple division,
each a city, and these are called by their names.

There, as sweet deliverance after the bitterness of misfortune,
to Tlepolemos, Tirynthian arch-founder, is given
as to a god
the smoking processional of sheep, the judgment of games, in
whose flowers
Diagoras was wreathed twice. At the glorious Isthmos the
luck four times was his.
One win to crown another at Nemea, at rocky Athens.

The bronze at Argos knew him, the caldrons
in Arkadia and Thebes, the temperate games
Boiotians keep;
Pellana likewise. At Aigina he won six times, at Megara the
stone ballot
tells no alternate story. But Zeus father, brooding over
the peaks of Atabyrios, honor the set of the song Olmpion-
ician,

the man who has found excellence with his fists. Grant him
pleasure of veneration
in the sight of citizens and strangers his friends. The path
estranged from violence
he walks straitly, sure of all that the upright minds of his
fathers
left, his heritage. Founder not the seed
of Kallianax, your own. With good fortune for the Eratidai
the city
has also its part of happiness. But in one parcel of time
the winds intershifting flare to new directions.

22

OLYMPIA 8

Mother of games, gold-wreathed, Olympia,
mistress of truth where men of prophecy
by burning victims probe the pleasure of Zeus of the shining
  thunderbolt,
what story he has for folk
who strain in spirit to capture
magnificence of strength
and space to breathe after work's weariness:

his will is steered by men's prayers to favor of piety.
Then, O grove of Pisa beside Alpheos, shadowed with trees,
accept this our festival song with its burden of garlands.
  Great is his fame forever
whom your bright victory befalls.
Various goods have come
to one man and another; there are many roads
to happiness, if the gods assent.

Timosthenes, destiny has assigned you and your brother
to Zeus Genethlios. He gave you glory at Nemea;
Alkimedon beside the Kronian hill
he made Olympic champion.
Splendid he was to behold, and, in action not shaming his
  beauty,
he won at wrestling to herald his homeland, Aigina of the
  sweeping oar.
There, beyond men elsewhere, they cultivate
her who sits beside Zeus of hospitality, Themis,

lady of salvation. With right wit to distinguish
that which has large and various weight in the scale, with-
  out failure,

is hard; yet some statute of the immortals has made this sea-
  girt land also
to strangers from all far places
a wonderful column of safety;
may time, uprolling, falter
never in accomplishment of that end.

Since Aiakos it was under stewardship of a Dorian people.
That hero Leto's son and Poseidon, wide-ranging of mind
in purpose to put a wreath of towers on Ilion, called to their
  aid
for the wall whose doom had been written,
how in the upsurge of war,
in the battle to storm the citadel,
smoke of destruction must blaze its end.

And at its first establishment three pale snakes
writhed aloft that rampart. Two, collapsing
overborne, gave up their lives.
One reared up with a cry.
Apollo, pondering the portent before him, spoke:
"Hero, Pergamos shall be taken where your hands have
  wrought.
So speaks to me this vision sent
by Kronos' deep-thundering son, even Zeus.

Nor without help of your children after you; it shall be
  broken
in the first and fourth generation." With this plain word the
  god
made for Xanthos urgently, and the well-horsed Amazons,
  and Ister.
The shaker of the trident steered to the sea's
Isthmos his running chariot,
bearing Aiakos home
aloft on his golden car

to visit the yoke of Korinth with its glorious feasting.
No single joy among men will match another's.
If, for the fame he has won with beardless boys, my song
   makes much of Melesias,
let no rancor cast at me a rugged stone.
I can speak of this same gladness
that came to him at Nemea
and thereafter in the men's contests

as pancratiast. It is better to know what you teach
if you teach it; not to study beforehand is thoughtless.
The minds of men untried are flimsy rather.
He better than others can expound
wrestling, the skill to further a man on his way
who out of sacred games would win the most desirable honor.
Now Alkimedon brings to him
with a thirtieth victory, praise.

By luck that comes from the gods and no failure of nerve
he forced on four boys' bodies
homecoming in bitterness, speech without honor, a secret
   path;
but into his sire's father inspired
strength to grapple his old age.
A man achieving the things desired
makes Hades to be forgotten.

But I must waken memory and bespeak
for the Blepsiadai success in the flowering strength of their
   hands.
Now is laid along their brows the sixth wreath from the
   leaves of contests.
Even they that are dead have some share
of things done in the true way;
nor does the dust obscure
the grace of their kinsmen's virtue.

Iphion, giving ear to Angelia, daughter of Hermes,
might speak to Kallimachos of the shining
glory at Olympia Zeus granted
them and theirs. May he will to bestow noble success
on nobility, fending aside the bitter edge of infirmity.
I pray him that destiny be of no doubtful counsel over
    these good men's fate,
but bring a life untroubled of grief
to bless themselves and their city.

OLYMPIA 9

The Archilochos song
cried aloud at Olympia, the victor hailed in his glory three
   times over
was enough by the Kronian hill to lead in triumph
Epharmostos in revelry with his beloved companions.
But now shower from the Muses' bows that range into wide
   distance,
Zeus, lord of the light in the red thunderbolt,
and with even such arrows
the solemn headland of Elis
that the hero Lydian Pelops of old
won, fairest bridal dower of Hippodameia.

Cast a winged shaft of delight
to Pytho likewise; you will find words that falter not to the
   ground
as you throb the lyre for a man and a wrestler
from famed Opous. Praise the land and her son.
Themis and the lady of salvation, Eunomia, her daughter,
the glorious, keep it for their own; he blossoms in exploits,
Kastalia, beside your spring
and by Alpheos river,
to make the garlands in their bloom lift up
the mother of Lokrian men, land of trees shining.

And I, lighting a city beloved
with blaze of whirling song,
swifter than the proud horse
or winged ship on the sea
will carry the message,
if with hand blessed I garden
this secret close of the Graces.

27

It is they who minister delightful things. If men are brave, or
  wise, it is by the divinity

in them; how else could Herakles'
hands have shaken the club against the trident
when by Pylos' gate Poseidon stood over against him,
and Phoibos strode on him with the silver bow in his hands
  poised;
neither the death-god Hades rested the staff
wherewith he marshals mortal bodies of men perished
down the hollow street. But, my lips,
cast this story from us.
For to revile the gods
is hateful learning, and to vaunt against season carries

an underweb of madness.
Speak not idly such things; let be war and all discord
apart from the immortals. Rather to Protogeneia's city
bring our speech, where, by decree of Zeus of the rippling
  thunder,
Deukalion and Pyrrha, coming down from Parnassos,
founded their house at the first and with no act of love estab-
  lished
a stone generation to be their folk.
These were named people therafter.
Wake for them the high strain of song,
and praise old wine, but the blossoms of poetry

that is young. For they say
the black earth was awash
under the weight of water; but by
Zeus' means, of a sudden the ebb-tide
drained the flood. And from these
came your ancestors, men with brazen shields,
traced back at the outset
to Iapeton's seed, sons of his daughters by the great sons of
  Kronos, kings in the land for all time

until the lord of Olympos,
ravishing from the Epeian land Opous' daughter, lay with
  her
secretly on Mainalian slopes; and thereafter he brought her
to Lokros, lest age, overtaking, doom him
to be childless. The bride carried the mighty
seed; and the hero was glad to see the son for his fostering.
He named him after his mother's sire,
to be called Opous,
a man surpassing in stature and action,
and gave him the city and the people to govern.

There came to him stranger-guests
from Argos and Thebes, Arkadians and Pisatans.
But beyond all newcomers he honored Aktor's son and Ai-
  gina's
Menoitios; he whose child, brought with the sons of Atreus,
in the plain of Teuthras stood his ground alone with Achilles
when Telephos, bending back the rest of the valiant Danaans,
hurled them against their own beached ships.
Thus was made plain for any
with wit to see how strong the heart of Patroklos;
and Thetis' son ordained thereafter that never

in grim battle should Patroklos be
marshaled apart from his own
man-wrecking spear's place.
May I find words now to win through
riding the car of the Muses
to the occasion. May daring and compassing power
come upon me. I went, in virtue of proxeny,
to stand by Lampromachos in his garlands of Isthmos, where
  both men won

on a single day their events.
And twice thereafter delight of victory came to him at the
  gates

of Korinth, as in the Nemean valley to Epharmostos.
He likewise at Argos won glory among men, and as a boy
at Athens; in Marathon, torn from beardless antagonists,
he stood the onset of older men for the silver vessels.
He threw these in his speed and craft
with no fall scored against him
and walked through the ring to loud acclamation
in the pride of his youth, splendid, and with achievement of
    splendor.

Before the Parrhasians assembled,
he appeared, a wonder, at the festival of Zeus Lykaios;
as when he won the cloak, warm medicine
of cold winds, at Pellene; the tomb of Iolaos
witnesses to his shining glory, as Eleusis the sea-borne.
Best by nature is best; but many have striven before now
to win by talents acquired
through art the glory.
But the thing unblessed by God is none
the worse for silence, always. There are ways

that surpass others.
But no one discipline sustains
us all. And skills are steep things
to win. As you bring the games' prize,
be bold to cry aloud
this man that is blessed by nature,
strong of hand, nimble, with eyes of valor,
who at your feast, Aias, son of Oileus, has wreathed your altar
    in victory.

Read the name of the conqueror, Olympian
son of Archestratos, where it is written down
on my heart. I owed him a sweet strain of music and forgot.
  O Muse and Truth,
daughter of Zeus, with steady hands
lift me back from the lies
and the reproach of bad friendship.

Stealing from afar upon me, time delayed
has shamed the depth of my debt.
Still, interest has strength to solve blame's bitterness; see how
  the wave, running, rolls
the stream-pebble along
and how we shall settle this debt
between us, the way of grace, as friends.

For the goddess of strict truth steers the city of the West
  Wind Lokrians,
and the Muse of heroes is among them,
and brazen Ares. The fight with Kyknos turned back even
  the surpassing might
of Herakles; and Agesidamos, winner
in boxing at Olympia,
may give thanks to Ilas his trainer, as once
to Achilles, Patroklos.
Sharpening one born for great achievement,
a man, under God's hand aiding, could drive to gigantic
  glory.

But, without striving, few have won joy of victory
to be a light upon their lifetime for all deeds accomplished.
The rights of Zeus are urgent with me to sing that pride of
  contests that Herakles by the primeval grave of Pelops

founded sixfold for his labors
when he had slain Poseidon's son,
the perfect fighter, Kteatos,

and slain Eurytos, in will to extract from Augeas
unwilling the mighty price of his lackey-service.
Lurking in ambush under Kleonai, Herakles smote them by
    the wayside,
since aforetime they had shattered
his following, the men of Tiryns,
as they lay in the deep places of Elis,

these Moliones in their high pride. The king of the Epeians,
treacherous to his very guest-friends, not long
thereafter saw his own rich city under stark fire
and the stroke of iron settling into the deep
pit of destruction.
No man can fend aside
the onset of stronger men.
Augeas also, at the last, in his fool's counsel
was taken and dragged to the edge of steep death, nor
    escaped it.

But the strong son of Zeus at Pisa,
gathering together his host and all their spoil,
ordained the grove sacred to his father, and fixed the Altis
    about in a clean place;
and a level floor circle-wise
he dedicated to be the banquet place,
doing honor to the Alpheus crossing

with the twelve gods who are lords; he named
the hill of Kronos. Before this,
under sway of Oinomaos, nameless it had been sunk under
    deep snow; and at this festival birth
the Fates were attendant, with him
who alone makes apparent
truth and that which things are,

Time. Who in his sweep forward has made plain
the way of the battle gift
and the division Herakles made of his war-spoil, the sacrifice,
   how he established
with this first Olympiad the five-year festival
and with prizes for games won.
Who, then, was given
the young wreath of victory
for his hands' work, or speed of foot, or chariot,
putting before his eyes the games' glory and accomplishing
   thought in action?

In the furlong race, keeping the strain of his running
in an even course, Likymnios' son,
Oionos, who came from Midea with his people; in the
   wrestling Echemos brought Tegea acclaim.
At boxing it was Doryklos won his way,
who dwelt in the city of Tiryns.
Guiding four horses abreast, Samos

of Mantinea, Halirothios' son.
Phrastor threw the spear to the limit;
but, whirling the stone disk in his hand, Nikeus spun a
   length beyond all others, and his fellowship
burst into uproar of acclamation. Into that evening
the winsome light of a moon,
full blown, burned on.

And every precinct in that glad celebration was filled with
   song,
in the mode of victory strains.
In the path of which ancient traditions, now also, for grace
in this namesake and exalting victory, we shall sing the
   thunder
and the fire-handed bolt
of Zeus of the loud stroke,

who, in strength, forever
grips the blazing thundershaft;
and the strain of song ripening shall meet melodies of the
reed flute

that came to light long since by famed Dirke.
Yet as his wife's child comes desirable
to a father who goes the way backward from youth, and with
great love makes warm his heart;
for wealth that is given an alien,
brought from without to master,
is a bitterness upon him who dies and leaves it;

so also, Agesidamos, a man who has done splendid things
without song, goes down into the courts of death
and has breathed out his might in empty endeavor, and got
brief joy. For you, the fair-spoken lyre
and the delicate flute drench you in beauty.
Wide is your honor, kept
by the maiden Pierides, Zeus' children.

And I, laying my hand strongly, have come to embrace
the famed men of Lokris, with honey
perfuming their city of good men. I have praised the beau-
tiful son
of Archestratos. I saw him win by strength of his hand
beside the Olympian altar
on that day long ago,
a splendor to behold,
and with that youth upon him that once
by the Kyprian's power delivered Ganymede from death the
shameless.

OLYMPIA 11

There is a time when men need most favoring
gales; there is a time for water from the sky,
rain, child of cloud.
But if by endeavor a man win fairly, soft-spoken songs
are given, to be a beginning of men's
speech to come and a true seal on great achievements.

Abundant is such praise laid up for victories
Olympian. My lips have good will
to marshal these words; yet only
by God's grace does a man blossom in the wise turning of his
    thought.
Son of Archestratos, know
that for the sake, Agesidamos, of your boxing

I shall enchant in strain of song a glory upon
your olive wreath of gold
and bespeak the race of the West Wind Lokrians.
There acclaim him; I warrant you,
Muses, you will visit no gathering cold to strangers
nor lost to lovely things
but deep to the heart in wisdom, and spearmen also. No
    thing, neither devious fox
nor loud lion, may change the nature born in his blood.

OLYMPIA 12

Daughter of Zeus who sets free, I beseech you, Fortune,
lady of salvation, guard the wide strength of Himera.
By your power are steered fleet ships on the sea,
sudden wars by land, the gatherings heavy
with counsel. Men's hopes, oft in the air,
downward rock again as they shear a heaving sea of lies.

Never yet has a man who walks upon earth
found from God sure sign of the matter to come.
Perception of future goes blind.
Many things fall counter to judgment, sometimes
against delight, yet others that encountered evil
gales win in a moment depth of grandeur for pain.

Son of Philanor, like a cock that fights at home
by his own hearth, even so the splendor
of your feet might have dropped to obscurity, had not
strife that sets men at odds cost you your homeland, Knossos.
Now, Ergoteles, garlanded at Olympia,
twice at Pytho, at the Isthmos, here at your new home,
Himera, you magnify in fame the Bathing Place of the
    Nymphs.

OLYMPIA 13

Thrice Olympionician
the house I praise, gentle to fellow-citizens,
ministrant to strangers. I will know
Korinth the rich, forecourt
of Poseidon of the Isthmos, shining in its young men.
There Law, sure foundation-stone of cities, dwells with
    Justice
and Peace, dispenser of wealth to man, her sisters,
golden daughters of Themis, lady of high counsels.

They will to drive afar
Pride, the rough-spoken, mother of Surfeit.
I have fair things to say, and straightforward
courage urges my lips to speak.
It is vain striving to hide inborn nature.
To you, sons of Alatas, the Hours have brought many times
    bright victory,
as in high achievement you ascended in the sacred contests,
even as, blossoming, they have founded in men's minds

the beginning of many a wise device, from you. To the
    inventor the deed belongs.
Where else did the graces of Dionysos
shine forth with the dithyramb ox-driven?
Who else put curbs to the gear of horses
or set pediments like the double eagle, lord of birds, on the
    gods'
temples? Among you the Muse, sweet-spoken,
among you Ares also,
flowers in your young men's spears of terror.

Lord on high, wide ruling
over Olympia, Zeus father,
begrudge not in all time these words;
and, guiding clear of disaster these people,
for Xenophon steer the wind of his destiny.
Take in his name this festival measure of garlands that he
   brings from the lawn of Pisa,
winner at once in pentathlon and the stade run; a thing
no mortal has matched in time before.

When he came forward at Isthmos,
two wreaths of parsley shaded him.
Nemea will tell no other story.
For Thessalos his father the shining glory
of speed in his feet is laid up by Alpheos' stream,
and at Pytho he had honor in one sun's course of the stade
   and the two-lap race; in the selfsame month
at Athens of the rocks one fleet-running day
laid wreaths of loveliness for three successes on his locks.

Seven times at the maid Hellotis' contests. In the field of
   Poseidon by the sea
for Terpsias and Eritimos with their father
Ptoiodoros, there are songs too long for my singing.
But for all your success at Delphoi
and in the Lion's meadow, I dispute with the rest
the multitude of your splendors. Yet in truth
even I have not power to number
surely the pebbles in the sea.

To each thing belongs
its measure. Occasion is best to know.
I in my own right have sailed with the multitude
and cry aloud the wisdom of your forefathers,
their warcraft in heroic courage
without lies that touch Korinth: Sisyphos most skilled of
   hand, as a god is;

Medeia, who ordained her marriage even in her father's
    despite,
savior of the ship Argo and her seamen;

the show of valor they made
long ago, before the Dardanian battlements,
on either side hewing to the end of strife;
these with the beloved sons of Atreus,
striving to win back Helen; those guarding her
amain. The Danaans shook before Glaukos, who came from
    Lykia. Before them
he vaunted that in the city of Peirene the power abode
and the deep domain and the house of Bellerophon, his fore-
    father,

who beside the Springs, striving to break the serpent Gor-
    gon's child,
Pegasos, endured much hardship
until the maiden Pallas gave him
the bridle gold-covered. Out of dream
there was waking, and she spoke: "Do you sleep, king de-
    scended of Aiolos?
Behold, take this magic for the horse
and dedicate to the father who tames
beasts, a shining bull in sacrifice."

To his dream in darkness
the girl of the black shield seemed to speak
such things, and he sprang upright on his feet.
Gathering up the strange thing that lay beside him,
he sought out, delighted, the prophet in the land
and showed Koiranides all the ending of the matter, how he
    had slept
that night, at his behest, by the goddesses' altar. How the very
    child
of Zeus of the thunder-spear had given into

his hands the conquering gold.
The seer bade him obey
in speed the dream; and, when he had immolated
a bull to him who grips the earth in his wide strength,
to found straightway an altar of Athene of the horses.
God's power makes light possession of things beyond oath
    or hope.
Strong Bellerophon, pondering, caught
with the quiet device drawn to the jaw

the winged horse. Riding, he made weapon play in full
    armor of bronze.
So mounted, out of the cold gulfs
of the high air forlorn, he smote
the archered host of women, the Amazons;
and the Chimaira, breathing flame; and the Solymoi, and
    slew them.
On his fate at the last I will keep silence.
But to Pegasos were given on Olympos
the lordly mangers of Zeus.

It becomes me not, spinning
the shaft's straight cast beside the mark, to speed
too many bolts from my hand's strength.
For I came fain helper to the Muses
on their thrones of shining, and to the Oligaithidai.
In brief word I will illumine their assembled success at Isth-
    mos and Nemea; and the lordly
herald's sworn glad cry of truth will bear witness
they conquered sixty times in these places.

It has beseemed me before this
to speak of all they have done at Olympia.
Things yet to come shall be told clear as they befall.
Even now I am full of hope, but the end lies
in God. If only his natal divinity walk far,

we shall bring this duty to Zeus and Ares. Under the brow
   of Parnassos there were six
wins; as many at Argos, in Thebes; the king's altar of Zeus
Lykaios will bespeak as many gained in Arkadian gorges;

Pellana and Sikyon, Megara, the fenced grove of the Aiaki-
   dai,
Eleusis and Marathon the shining,
the rich cities in their loveliness under the crest of Aitna,
Euboia also; stir with your hand
all Hellas, they will rise to outpass the eyes' vision.
Let me swim out with light feet.
Zeus accomplisher, to all grant grave restraint
and attainment of sweet delight.

OLYMPIA 14

You who have your dwelling
in the place of splendid horses, founded beside the waters of
   Kephisos:
O queens of song and queens of shining
Orchomenos: Graces: guardians of the primeval Minyai,
hear! My prayer is to you. By your means all delight,
all that is sweet, is given to mankind.
If a man be wise, or beautiful, or splendid, it is you.
Without the grave Graces, not the gods even
marshal their dances, their festivals; mistresses of all
heavenly action, they who have set their thrones
beside Pythian Apollo of the bow of gold
keep eternal the great way of the father Olympian.

Lady and mistress Aglaia,
and Euphrosyne, delighting in song, daughters of the greatest
god, hear me now; and Thalia,
lover of dancing, as you look down, with fortune favorable,
   on this victory throng
stepping delicately. For I have come to Asopichos
with song worked carefully to the Lydian measure,
because the Minyan land has been made triumphant at
   Olympia
by your grace, Lady. Go now, Echo, to the black wall
of the house of Persephone, bring to his father the clear mes-
   sage;
stand in the presence of Kleodamos and say that his son
in the renowned valley of Pisa
has put on his young hair the wings of glory for games won.

PYTHIA 1

Golden lyre, held of Apollo in common possession
with the violet-haired Muses: the dance steps, leaders of
    festival, heed you;
the singers obey your measures
when, shaken with music, you cast the beat to lead choirs of
    dancers.
You have power to quench the speared thunderbolt
of flowing fire. Zeus' eagle sleeps on his staff, folding his
    quick wings both ways to quiet,

lord of birds; you shed a mist on his hooked head,
dark and gentle closure of eyes; dreaming, he ripples
his lithe back, bound in spell
of your waves. Violent Ares even, leaving aside the stern
    pride
of spears, makes gentle his heart in sleep.
Your shafts enchant the divinities by grace of the wisdom of
    Lato's son and the deep-girdled Muses.

Yet such creatures as Zeus loves not are shaken to hear
the music of the Pierides, whether on earth or the sea unrest-
    ing;
likewise he who sprawls, God's enemy, in the pit of Tartaros,
Typhon, the hundred-headed, whom of old
the cave of many names in Kilikia bred; and now
the sea-dykes above Kymai are set over him;
Sicily crushes his shaggy
chest; the sky's pillar is piled above him,
Aitna of the snows, year-long
minister of the cleaving ice.

43

Thence erupt pure founts of unapproachable fire
from the secret places within; by day the rivers spout in a
    flood of smoke,
shot through with shining; by dark from the rock
the red flame rolling plunges to the deep sea-plain in tumult.
The monster hurls aloft such spouts
of weird flame; a portent and a wonder to behold, a wonder
    even to hear from those who have seen.

Thus, beneath the pinnacles dark in leaves of Aitna he lies
    shackled
underground, and the jagged bed rips all his back that is
    cramped against it.
May it be our lot, Zeus, rather to please you.
You are lord of this mountain, forefront of a bountiful land,
    and in its name
a famous founder has made glorious the city beside it
when in the Pythian field the herald cried aloud, announcing
    Hieron's splendor of victory

in the chariot race. For men who would take ship first grace
is a favoring wind to befall the passage begun; there is like to
    follow
at the last also a better homecoming therefor; and calculation
upon these things befallen brings hope
that this city hereafter will be famed for garlands won with
    its horses,
and in the singing festivals be a place renowned.
Lykian and lord of Delos,
Apollo, who love Parnassos also and the Kastalian spring,
may it please you to bring these things to pass
and to make this country one blessed in its manhood.

From the gods come all means to mortal endeavor;
by them we are wise, or strong with our hands, or eloquent
    of speech; and I, pondering

praise of Hieron, have hope
not, like a thrower, hefting the bronze-shod spear to fling it
    wide of the course,
but with a far cast to beat my antagonists.
If only the rest of his time might keep firm such wealth and
    possession of goods, and bring also forgetfulness of his
    labors.

So might he remember in what onsets of battle
he stood with enduring heart, when these men found at the
    gods' hands honor
such as reaps no Hellene else,
a garland of wealth to make men proud. Now in truth he
    takes Philoktetes' way
of war; and in constraint even the proud man
fawns on his friendship. They say that godlike heroes came
    to bring Poias' son, the mighty archer,

from Lemnos, where he lay in pain of his festering wound;
and he sacked Priam's city and made an end of the Danaans'
    labors;
he came with flesh infirm, but a man of doom.
In such wise may God guide Hieron
in the time that steals upon us, granting him occasion of all
    he longs for.
Muse, be governed by me to sing
for Deinomenes requital of the chariot victory.
The joy of his father's triumph is no stranger to him.
Let us find for the king of Aitna
some splendor of song that shall be his own.

For him Hieron founded that city in liberty built
of gods, and ordinances of Hyllos' rule, and the descendants
    of Pamphylos,
those, too, of Herakles' seed,
who dwell beside Taygetos' slopes, are minded to abide for-
    ever in the decrees of Aigimios,

Dorians. These were blessed in Amyklai's taking;
they rose and went from Pindos to dwell, deep in glory, next
   to the Tyndaridai, and the fame of their spears has blos-
   somed.

Zeus accomplisher, beside the waters of Amenas forever
let all men's speech decree such praise on the citizens and
   their kings.
By your aid, this leader of men,
enjoining it upon his son also, might glorify his people and
   turn them to peace and harmony.
Kronion, I beseech you, bend your head in assent
that the Phoenician and the war-crying Tyrsenian keep
   quietly at home, beholding the shame of their wreck by
   sea at Kyme,

the things they endured, beaten at the hands of Syracuse's
   lord,
how he hurled their young men out of their fleet-running
   ships on the sea,
gathering back Hellas from the weight of slavery. I am given
favor in requital from men of Athens for Salamis
battle, and in Sparta for the fighting before Kithairon,
where the Medes, benders of the bow, went under;
so likewise for singing fulfilment
for Deinomenes' sons of their victory at the watered strand
   of Himera,
that which they won by valor
when their foemen were beaten down.

Singing in season and drawing narrow the strands
of many matters, you will find less mockery of men that
   follows. Sad surfeit blunts
the speed of flying hopes.
If citizens hear overmuch of the bliss of others, it galls the
   secrecy of their hearts.

Nevertheless, for envy outshines pity,
pass not over splendid things. With a just tiller steer your
   host. Forge your speech on an anvil that rings no falsehood.

A spark of dross flying is called a great matter
coming from you. You are steward of many, and many are
   the witnesses for good or ill who shall be believed.
Abide in this flowering temper,
and, if you would hear speech of delight always, falter not in
   your bounty.
Let go, like a pilot, your sails
free to the wind. Be not beguiled, dear friend, by easy profit.
   The vaunt of reputation to come

alone controls the way men speak of those that are gone, their
   life
in song and story. The generous achievement of Kroisos fades
   not.
But hateful everywhere is the speech that oppresses Phalaris,
the heart without pity, who roasted men in the bronze bull.
Nor lyres under the roof welcome him
as the sweet theme for the voices of boys singing.
Good fortune is first of prizes,
and good repute has second place; the man who attains
these two and grasps them in his hands
is given the uttermost garland.

PYTHIA 2

Great city, O Syracuse, precinct of Ares
who haunts the deeps of battle; nurse divine of horses and
    men that fight in iron,
from shining Thebes I come, bringing you
this melody, message of the chariot course that shakes the
    earth,
wherein Hieron in success of his horses
has bound in garlands that gleam far Ortygia,
site of the river-Artemis, whose aid stood not afar
when, with gentling hands, he guided the intricate reins of
    his young mares.

For the lady of arrows, in both hands bestowing,
and Hermes of the contests set the gleam of glory on his
    head, when to the polished car
and the harness he yokes temperate strength
of horses, invoking also the god of wide strength who shakes
    the trident.
For other kings aforetime other men also have given
the high sound of song, requital of their achievement.
Incessantly the Kyprian songs are of Kinyras,
beloved of the gold-haired god, Apollo, in fulness of heart,

and sacred in the favor of Aphrodite. Grace of friendship
in courteous gaze comes also to bless in requital deeds done.
Son of Deinomenes,
the West Lokrian maiden
at her doors speaks of you; and her gaze, by grace of your
    might,
goes now untroubled, after the hopeless struggles of war-
    time.
It is by gods' work that they say Ixion,
fixed on his winged wheel, spun in a circle,

cries aloud this message to mortals:
To your benefactor return ever with kind dealing rendered.

He learned that lesson well. By favor of the sons of Kronos,
he was given a life of delight but could not abide blessedness
    long; in his delirious heart
he loved Hera, dedicated to the high couch
of Zeus. That outrage hurled him into conspicuous
ruin. He was a man and endured beyond all others
distress full merited. Two sins flowered
to pain in his life: a hero, he first
infected the mortal breed with kindred bloodshed, not with-
    out treachery;

also, in the great secret chambers of Zeus he strove to ravish
the Queen. A man should look at himself and learn well his
    own stature.
The coupling unnatural brought accumulation of evil
on him, even in success; it was a cloud he lay with,
and he in his delusion was given the false loveliness.
A phantom went in the guise of that highest daughter
of Uranian Kronos; a deceit visited upon him
by the hands of Zeus, a fair evil thing. Zeus likewise wrought
    the crucifixion on the wheel,

Ixion's bane; and, spinning there, limbs fast
to the ineluctable circle, he makes the message a thing that
    all may know.
But she, graceless, spawned
a child of violence.
There was none like her, nor her son; no honor was his
    portion in the usage of god or man.
Nursing him, she named him Kentauros, and he coupled
with the Magnesian mares on the spurs of Pelion;
and a weird breed was engendered
in the favor of either parent:
the mare's likeness in the parts below, and the manlike father
    above.

49

It is God that accomplishes all term to hopes,
God, who overtakes the flying eagle, outpasses the dolphin
in the sea; who bends under his strength the man with
   thoughts too high,
while to others he gives honor that ages not. My necessity
is to escape the teeth of reproach for excessive blame.
Standing afar, I saw Archilochos the scold,
laboring helpless and fattening on his own cantankerous
hate, naught else; prosperity, blessed with fortune, gives the
   highest wisdom.

You, in freedom of your heart, can make this plain,
you, that are prince of garlanded streets in their multitude
   and lord of the host. If any man
claims that, for possession of goods and high honor,
some other of those that lived of old in Hellas has overpassed
   you,
that man with loose heart wrestles emptiness.
I shall mount the wreathed ship to speak aloud
your praise. Your youth is staunch in valor to endure
stark battle; whence I say you have found glory that knows
   no measure

in striving against those who rode horses in battle
and the fighting footranks also. But your elder counsels
set me free to speak forth
in your praise, a word without peril
against any man's contention. Hail, then! This melody is
   sent you
like Phoenician ware over the gray sea.
Be fain to behold and welcome the Kastor-chant
on Aiolian strings, by grace
of the seven-stringed lyre.
Learn what you are and be such. See, the ape to children is a
   pretty thing, pretty indeed.

But Rhadamanthys has done well, to reap
a blameless harvest of the mind, without joy of deception at
    the inward heart,
such as ever befalls a man by action of those who whisper.
To both sides the speakers of slander are an evil beyond
    control.
They are minded like foxes, utterly.
But what good then befalls the greedy fox of his slyness?
As when the rest of the gear founders in the sea's
depth, I, the cork at the net, ride not drenched in the brine.

But the treacherous citizen has no force to cast a word of
    power
among the great. Still, fawning on all, he threads his way
    too far.
His confidence is not mine. Be it mine to love my friend,
but against the enemy, hateful indeed, turn with the wolf's
    slash,
treading, as the time may need, my devious path.
Yet in each state the candid man will go far,
when tyrants rule, or the swirling rabble,
or the wise keep the city in ward. Yet, it is ill to strive with
    God

who upholds now one faction, now to the other gives
great glory. Even success softens not the heart
of the envious. Straining
as it were at a pegged line
too far, they stab the spike to rend their own hearts
before attainment of the desire in their minds.
To bear lightly the neck's yoke
brings strength; but kicking
against the goads is the way
of failure. Be it mine that good men will to have me among
    their friends.

PYTHIA 3

I could wish that Chiron, Philyra's son
(if such word of prayer from my lips could be published),
the departed, were living yet,
child wide-minded of Uranian Kronos, and ruled the Pelian
   glades, that beast of the hills
with the heart kindly to men, as of old when he reared
the gentle smith of pain's ease to heal bodies, Asklepios,
the hero who warded sickness of every kind.

Koronis, daughter of Phlegyas the rider,
before with the ministration of Eleithyia she brought her
   child to birth, was stricken
by the golden bow of Artemis
and went down into the house of death from her chamber,
   by design of Apollo. No slight thing
is the anger of the children of Zeus. She, forgetting him
in her confused heart, accepted a second marriage, in secrecy
   from her father,
she who had lain before with Phoibos of the loose hair

and carried the immaculate seed of the god.
She could not stay for the coming of the bride-feast,
not for hymen cry in many voices, such things
as the maiden companions of youth are accustomed to sing
at nightfall, using the old names of endearment. No.
She was in love with what was not there; it has happened to
   many.
There is a mortal breed most full of futility.
In contempt of what is at hand, they strain into the future,
hunting impossibilities on the wings of ineffectual hopes.

The will of delicately robed Koronis held
this sin of pride. For she lay in bed with a stranger
that came from Arkadia, nor escaped
the Watcher. In his temple at Pytho, where the sheep are
   offered, King Loxias knew,
persuading his heart to the sheerest witness, his own
mind that knows all; he has no traffic with lies, nor god
nor man escapes him in purpose or deed of the hand.

Knowing the hospitality of bed given Ischys,
Eilatos' son, and the graceless treachery, he sent his sister,
   inflamed
with anger that brooked no bar,
to Lakereia, for the girl lived by Boibias under the pendulous
   cliffs; her angel
shifted to evil and struck her down; and many a neighbor
shared, and was smitten together. Fire on a mountain leaping
from one seed will obliterate a great forest.

But when her kinsmen had laid the girl in the wall
of wood, and Hephaistos' greedy flame
ran high, then spoke Apollo: "No longer
will I endure in my heart the destruction of my own child
by death in agony for the weight of his mother's punish-
   ment."
He spoke, and in the first stride was there and caught the boy
from the body, and the blaze of the pyre was divided before
   him.
Carrying him to the centaur in Magnesia, he gave him to be
   perfected
in the healing of sickness that brings many pains to men.

They came to him with ulcers the flesh had grown,
or their limbs mangled with the gray bronze, or bruised
with the stone flung from afar,
or the body stormed with summer fever, or chill; and he
   released each man and led him

from his individual grief. Some he treated with guile of
   incantations,
some with healing potions to drink; or he tended the limbs
   with salves
from near and far; and some by the knife he set on their feet
   again.

But even genius is tied to profit. Someone
turned even Asklepios with a winning price, showing the
   gold in his hand,
to bring back from death a man
already gone. But Kronion, with a cast of his hand, tore life
   from the hearts of both men
instantly, and the shining thunder dashed them to death.
With our mortal minds we should seek from the gods that
   which becomes us,
knowing the way of the destiny ever at our feet.

Dear soul of mine, never urge a life beyond
mortality, but work the means at hand to the end.
But if only temperate Chiron were living yet in his cave,
and the charm of these songs I make might have cast some
   spell
across his heart, I could have persuaded him even now
to give me a healer against the burning sickness of great men,
someone called son of Latoidas or even Zeus the father.
I could have come by ship cutting the Ionian sea
to the spring of Arethousa and my friend and host of Aitna.

He disposes in Syracuse as a king,
mild to citizens, not envious of good men, to strangers a
   father admired.
If I could have come down from the sea
with a gift in either hand, golden health, and praise, glorious
   with garlands of the Pythian Games

Pherenikos won him long ago, the best horse beside Kirrha,
I say that I would have crossed the deep sea bringing him
    light
to shine afar, more bright than a star in heaven.

But I will pray to the Great Mother
to whom night after night before my doors, a stately goddess,
the maidens dance, and to Pan beside her.
But, Hieron, if you know how to take the straight issue of
    words, you have seen from what came before:
For every one good thing the immortals bestow on men
two evils. Men who are as children cannot take this becom-
    ingly;
but good men do, turning the brightness outward.

The portion of happiness has come your way.
Great destiny looks to you, if to any man, as a lord
and leader of people. But a life unshaken
befell neither Peleus called Aiakidas
nor godlike Kadmos, yet men say these two were given
blessedness beyond all mortals. They heard on the moun-
    tain
and at seven-gated Thebes the gold-chapleted Muses singing
when one married ox-eyed Harmonia, and the other
wise Nereus' legendary daughter, Thetis.

And the gods feasted beside them each in turn,
and they saw the kings, the sons of Kronos, in their golden
    chairs, and accepted
their gifts. And after weariness of old
they won in requital the favor of Zeus, and their hearts were
    lifted. Yet in time
three daughters suffered and made Kadmos desolate
of gladness; though Zeus father came to the lovely embrace
of the fourth, white-armed Thyona.

And Peleus' son, the sole child
immortal Thetis bore him in Phthia, left life in battle, arrow-
    struck;
and his body, burned on the pyre,
stirred the Danaan grief. If any mortal keeps in mind the
    right road to truth, he must take
with grace whatever the gods give. Various ways go the
    blasts
of the high-flown winds. Men's prosperity will not walk far
safe, when it fares under its own deep weight.

I will be small in small things, great among great.
I will work out the divinity that is busy within my mind
and tend the means that are mine.
Might God only give me luxury and its power,
I hope I should find glory that would rise higher hereafter.
Nestor and Sarpedon of Lykia we know,
men's speech, from the sounding words that smiths of song
    in their wisdom
built to beauty. In the glory of poetry achievement of men
blossoms long; but of that the accomplishment is given to
    few.

PYTHIA 4

Today, my Muse, you must stand by a man beloved,
king of Kyrene, the city of noble horses; there at Arkesilas'
 festival
swell the wind of singing, the debt to Lato's children and
 Pytho,
where, throned beside the golden eagles of Zeus,
with Apollo himself not far, the priestess
prophesied that Battos should come to colonize the corn-
 lands of Libya,
leaving his sacred island to found a city
of chariots at the shining breast of the sea;

that he must bring home at last
in the seventeenth generation, Medeia's word, that Aietes'
mantic daughter, lady of Kolchis, spoke of old with immortal
 lips at Thera. Her prophecy
to the half-god crew of Jason the spearman:
"Hearken, children of high-hearted men and of gods.
I say to you that from this sea-beaten soil, Epaphos' daughter
Libya shall be planted, and made a stock beloved of cities
in Zeus Ammon's place of establishment.

"They shall change winged dolphins of the sea for running
 horses,
oars for reins, and steer chariots with storm in their feet.
That augury shall make Thera to be mother-city
of great populations, the prophecy spoken, where Triton's
 lake
pours to the sea, by a god in mortal guise; he offered earth,
and Euphamos, leaping down, accepted the token of friend-
 ship,
and over the portent Kronos' son, Zeus father, clashed his
 thunder.

"The god came as we slung the bronze-fanged
anchor aboard, fleet Argo's bridle. Twelve full days before
we had carried the sea-timber from Ocean's stream, over the
desolate ridges, at my behest heaving up the weight.
There the lonely divinity drew near, and upon him
was the shining appearance of a man august. He opened in
    words
of friendship, as those whereby men of kindness
proffer newcome outlanders entertainment.

"We spoke of the sweet necessity of return that stayed
our lingering. He named himself Eurypylos, son of the
    earthshaker immortal, Poseidon;
he understood our haste, but, tearing a clod from the soil,
proffered it in his right hand, a token of friendship.
The hero Euphamos disobeyed him not, but, vaulting ashore,
set hand in hand and accepted the magic piece of earth.
They tell me that, washed from the deck,
it has gone with the current,

"at nightfall down the salt sea's bending track. Indeed, over
    and again I charged
the grooms, easing their masters, to guard it well. But their
    hearts forgot.
And now the seed imperishable of wide
Libya is washed before its time to this island. But had Eu-
    phamos gone
home to sacred Tainaron and cast it down at the mortal gate
    of Hades,
he being lord and son of Poseidon, ruler of horses,
born of Tityos' daughter, Europa, beside the banks of
    Kephisos;

"in his children's fourth generation
his blood, with the Danaans' aid, had taken the broad con-
    tinent. For in that time

58

they shall be driven, and leave Lakedaimon and Argos bay
   and Mykenai.
As it is, he shall beget a race elect in the bed
of strange women; and thereafter, coming by God's ordi-
   nance to this
island, they shall bring forth a man to be lord of shadowy
   plains.
On a day to come, in the golden house,
as he approaches at last the Pythian shrine,

"Phoibos shall speak to him in words of prophecy
and bid him carry in ships cities to the rich demesne of
   Kronian Neilos."
Lo, the marshaled words of Medeia; and the godlike heroes
   were struck to motionless
silence, hearing the depth of her brooding thought.
O son of Polymnastos, blessed, by this decree
the oracle steered your course in the voice unasked of the
   winged priestess,
who, with threefold salutation, revealed you
destined king of Kyrene,

as you came to ask what release the gods might grant of your
   stammering voice.
And in after time, and now, as in the bright pride of flower-
   ing spring,
eighth in his generation, Arkesilas ripens to his prime,
and to him Apollo and Pytho have sped glory at the Amphik-
   tyons' hands
for his chariot victory. I give him now to the Muses
with the ram's fleece all of gold, in whose quest
the Minyans sailed, and honors bestowed of God were made
   to befall them.

What, then, was the beginning of their adventure?
What danger nailed them fast in the strength of steel? The
   word of God ran that Pelias

must die at the hands, or the unyielding contrivance, of some
   proud scion of Aiolos.
The stark prophecy came to his wary mind
spoken beside the naveled center of leafy Earth, our mother:
"Beware and hold in all guard him of the single sandal
when he comes down from the steep steadings
to the rising round of famed Iolkos,

stranger be he or citizen." And he came in his time,
a man terrible with twin javelins; and a twofold guise was
   on him.
A tunic of Magnesian fashion fitted close his magnificent
   limbs,
and across it a panther's hide held off the shivering rains.
Nor did the glory of his streaming locks go shorn,
but blazed the length of his back. Striding apace
he stood, and tested his unfaltering will
in the market place that filled with people.

They knew him not; yet awe-struck one man would say to
   another:
"This cannot be Apollo, surely, nor Aphrodite's lord,
he of the brazen chariot. And in shining Naxos they say
Iphimedeia's children died, Otos, and you, lord Ephialtes the
   reckless.
And Artemis' arrows, cast from the might of her quiver,
struck down Tityos in the speed of his desire,
that any man hereafter may long rather to catch at loves he
   has power to take."

So they questioned one another and made
answer. But with his polished car and mules Pelias urgently
drove up. He stared as he saw the sandal conspicuous
on the right foot, and there only. But, veiling the fear
in his heart, he spoke: "What manner of land, my friend,
might you claim as your own? What groundling woman let
   you forth

from a sere womb? See that you stain not your race
with lies, that to all men are most hateful."

He boldly but in speech of gentleness made answer:
"I think I can carry Chiron's discipline. For I come from his
    cave
and the side of Chariklo and Philyra, where the Centaur's
    stainless daughters brought me to manhood.
With twenty years gone to fulfilment and no deed
done, no word spoken to offend them, I have come
home, bringing back my father's lordship (administered
now by no right) that Zeus of old granted, privilege
of Aiolos, leader of men, and his sons thereafter.

"For I hear that Pelias, unrighteously and in persuasion of his
    pale heart,
has stripped the power by force from my fathers, the kings
    of old.
They, when I first saw light, fearing the proud
chief's violence, made dark mourning as if I had died
in the house; under the cloak of women's mingled
lamentation they sent me away in my splendid raiment;
they made their way by night and brought me to Chiron,
    Kronos' son, to be reared.

"But the heads of all these chapters you know well.
Point me now clearly, honored citizens, the house of my
    fathers, lords of white horses.
I am one of you, Aison's child, and this soil I tread is not
    alien.
And the divine beast when he spoke to me called me Jason."
He said; and his father's eyes, as he came in the house, knew
    him,
and tears gathered and fell from the withered eyelids
for joy in his heart, as he saw his chosen son
a man, and splendid beyond all others.

61

And from either side his two brothers
came at the rumor of him: from near at hand, Pheres, leaving
    the spring Hypereian,
and from far Messana, Amythaon; and with speed came
    Admetos also and Melampos
to their cousin's side. And in the feast's spell
with words of love Jason gave them entertainment,
appointing the feast of fellowship with all delight for these
    men
assembled, reaping five nights together and five days
the hallowed blossoming of life's luxury.

But on the sixth he laid all the urgent tale open from the
    beginning
to his kinsmen. And they followed his guidance. Suddenly
    from their benches
they sprang up, he and they together. They came to the hall
    of Pelias
and thronging strode within. At the noise of their coming
    he, lovely-haired
Tyro's child, stood forth to meet them. But Jason,
letting his voice flow gently into quiet discourse,
cast down the foundation-stone of wise argument: "Son of
    Poseidon

"of the Rock: the hearts of mortals are all too rapid
to take the crooked way of gain over righteousness, though
    they edge withal to the rough reckoning day.
But it beseems you and me, tempering our passion, to weave
    wealth in our time.
You know well what I mean. One dam mothered Kretheus
and reckless Salmoneus, whence, in the third generation
born, you and I gaze on the golden strength of the sun.
The very Fates, their faces veiled for shame, stand apart
before hatred growing among blood kinsmen.

62

"It is not for us by brazen edge of the sword
or with spears to divide our great patrimony. Behold: I
  release to you
the sheep, and all the tawny herds of cattle you wrested once
from my people, and administer to make fat your wealth.
It grieves me nothing that thereby you advanced your estate
  so far.
But the scepter of single rule and the throne, where Aison,
  Kretheus' son, in his sessions
made straight the dooms for a knightly multitude—
these, with no strife joined between us,

"surrender to me; lest you make some fresh disaster to rise."
He spoke, and mildly in his turn Pelias made answer: "Such
  a man
will I be. But the elder spell of life
is on me, while your youth gathers even now to its blossom-
  ing. You have strength to lift
the wrath of the undergods. Phrixos calls us to journey
to Aietes' house, and bring home his ghost
and the deep fleece of the ram whereby he fled death at sea

"and the godless weapons of his stepmother.
The weird dream-shape haunts me and speaks. And I have
  taken counsel at the shrine by Kastalia
what shift to make; the god's behest is in speed to appoint a
  sea-venture.
Take this endeavor upon yourself and achieve it; I swear
I will yield you the whole kingship. Let Zeus
of our fathers be witness, to bind us under a strong oath."
These two assenting to the compact were parted.
But Jason now in his own right

Sped heralds abroad with news of the voyage that was be-
  ginning.
In speed came three sons of Kronian Zeus, heroes wearied
  never in battle,

63

Alkmana's son and two by Leda of the glancing eyes; and
  two deep-haired men
sprung of Poseidon, heroes whose thoughts were of valor
from Pylos and the rock of Tainaron; thereby splendor
of glory was brought to fulfilment for Euphamos, and for
  you, Periklymenos the mighty.
And of Apollo's blood the harper came and father of lyric
voices, Orpheus the admired.

Hermes also of the golden staff sent twin sons on this labor
  relentless,
Erytos and Echion in the laughing pride of their youth. And
  two
that were swift came, dwellers beside the Pangaios pastures.
For of his own will and with heart favorable, Boreas, king
  of the winds,
their father, sent Zetes and Kalais, men with backs
ruffled to two red wings.
And Hera inflamed overpowering sweet desire in the demi-
  gods

for the ship Argo; lest any, left at home,
sit mulling beside his mother a life with no danger; rather
  against death even
they found the fairest defense that essence of valor in their
  own fellowship.
Such company, flower of seafarers, came down to the sea
  at Iolkos,
and Jason assembled them and admired all. The seer
Mopsos, making prophecy by birds and the sacred lots,
sent with good augury the host on board; and when
they had slung the anchors at the cutwater,

the leader, taking a golden bowl in his hands
at the stern, intreated Uranian Zeus our father, of the thun-
  derspear, invoked

fleet-running currents of the waves, winds, nights, and the
   sea's ways
and days to be favorable, and the dear doom of homecoming
   at the end.
And out of the clouds Zeus, answering, called back a mantic
peal of thunder; and the bright branches of sheer lightning
   broke in flame.
The heroes, trusting the signs apparent of God,
drew breath; and the prophet cried aloud,

bespeaking glad expectations, to bend to their sweeps;
and slakeless the oars went dipping from the speed in their
   hands.
On a following southwest wind they came to the Euxine
   mouth,
and founded there a holy precinct to the sea-god Poseidon,
and a red herd of Thracian bulls was dedicated
with the slab of an altar new-founded upon piled stones.
Straining now into deep danger, they supplicated the lord of
   ships

to escape the stark collision of the Clashing
Rocks. These were two, and alive; they rolled together with
   shock more fleet
than the battalions of thunderous winds; but even now that
   sailing
of demigods brought their death. To Phasis thereafter
they came, to meet in their strength the dark men of Kolchis
at the house of King Aietes. But Aphrodite, lady of Kypros,
mistress of rending arrows, sent down from Olympos the
   bright wryneck,
binding crosswise over a breakless wheel

the passionate bird, that was brought that time first
to mortal man; and she made Aisonides, Jason, wise in
   charm and incantation

that he might loosen Medeia's shame for her parents, and
    Hellas be all her desire,
that her heart ablaze under the lash of longing be set in
    tumult.
And she revealed forthwith the secret of the trials her father
    would set,
and with oil medicating simples against stark pain
gave them for his use. And they compacted marriage to be
joined thereafter in all delight between them.

Now when Aietes before them all had driven home the steel
    plowshare,
those oxen, that blew from their tawny jaws the flame of
    ravening fire
and tore the soil with brazen hoofs as they passed,
these he led and forced their necks to the yoke, single-handed;
    then, running the furrow straight,
drove, and ripped six feet deep the back of earth.
He spoke then: "Let the king, whoever he be,
lord of the ship, do this for me; then take away the robe
    unperishing,

"the bright fleece tasseled in gold."
He ended, and Jason, reliant on God, threw down his saffron
    mantle
and stepped to the work. Flame, by craft of the strange witch-
    maiden, harmed him not.
Gripping the plow, he bent the necks of the oxen under,
binding the yoke upon them, and by main strength of his
    shoulders,
with the fell goad laid on, plowed the whole length perforce.
Aietes, even in pained and speechless amazement,
gasped, admiring that act of strength;

and his friends held out their arms to the man in his might
and with leaf-woven garlands crowned him, and spoke him
    fair with admiring words.

Straightway Helios' wonderful son spoke of the shining
  fleece
where Phrixos' knife had flayed and hung it.
His hope was that not even so could the man accomplish that
  labor,
for it was set in a thicket, and guarded by the rending fangs
  of a great snake
that for measure and thickness outpassed a galley of fifty oars
the ax's stroke has labored to build.

The high road is long for me to travel, and time closes. I
  know
a short path, I that guide many another in the craft of singers.
By guile he slew the green-eyed serpent of the burnished
  scales,
O Arkesilas, and stole away Medeia, with her good will, she
  that was bane to Pelias.
They touched the gulfs of Ocean and the Red Sea,
and at Lemnos the breed of women that had slain their
  lords;
and there in games, for prize of raiment, displayed the
  strength in their limbs.

They lay with these women. And in this strange soil dropped,
day, or night season that was destined, took up the seed of
  your shining
wealth to come. There gendered the blood of Euphamos
  waxed
into the rest of time. These lived with the men of Lakedaimon
and in their ways; at last colonized the Lovely Island,
Thera; whence Apollo, Lato's son, has granted Libya's plain
  to be yours,
to make great in God's right, and the city divine
of golden-throned Kyrene to be administered

while you find wisdom yours to make counsel of righteous-
  ness.

Know now the wisdom of Oidipous: "If, with the cutting
  edge of the ax, men shear
the branches of a great oak, and defile its glorious symmetry,
spent though its issue be, it gives account of its worth
if it be brought at last to the winter fire
or with upright columns prop a palace
and shoulder the bitter burden in strange walls,
leaving its own place desolate."

But you are a healer in season, and Apollo Paian knows your
  glory.
You must tend the ulcered wound, laying a gentle hand on
  the place.
It is a light thing even for a weak man to shake a city,
but to set it again in place is a work of pain and strength,
  unless
God himself appear to set right the leaders.
For you gracious ends of these endeavors are weaving.
Be patient to work with full heart for the sake of Kyrene the
  blessed.

Read also this, the word of Homer,
and make it true; he said that a noble messenger brought
  highest honor to all things done.
The Muse is increased also by true interpretation. Kyrene
  knows,
and the storied hall of Battos, the just designs
of Damophilos. Among the youth he is a young man,
but in conclave an elder, as one that has met with a hundred
  years;
he bereaves the evil mouth of its clear outcry;
he has learned to loathe the violent man,

but against the noble he strives not, neither delays
accomplishment. Men's opportunity has the measure of a
  brief thing.

He knows this well; as a henchman he follows you, no slave.
  But they say
of all things this is bitterest, to know the right way, but be
  bound
by constraint of foot abroad. The great Atlas even now
struggles under the weight of the sky, far from his father's
  lands and his own possessions.
But Zeus immortal set free the Titans. With time
sails change as the winds die down.

His prayer is that, when he has drained to the lees his bitter
  affliction,
he may see home, and by Apollo's spring in the festival time
give over his heart to gladness often, and among his own
  people
that are wise lift up the elaborate lyre and touch the strings
  in peace,
devising no grief for any man, and himself not grieved by his
  fellows.
And he might tell you, Arkesilas, as a tale
the spring of immortal words he found of late as a guest in
  Thebes.

PYTHIA 5

Wide is the strength of Wealth
when, mixed with stainless virtue
and granted of destiny, mortal man leads it home,
most dear companion.
Arkesilas, God's destiny is on you;
from the towering stairs
of your renowned life
you approach it in glory
by Kastor's favor, of the golden chariot,
who, after storm of winter, makes
your hearth shine in the blessed quiet.

Even power granted of God
is carried the better for wisdom.
You walk in righteousness, and great prosperity is unceasing
    about you,
twice over: since you are king
of great cities,
for this high privilege
is a shining heritage in your house,
which matches your own temper;
and blessed are you even now, in that,
winning from the famed Pythiad success with horses, your
    prayer's end,
you are given this festal choir of men,

delight of Apollo; whereby, forget not,
as you are sung at Kyrene's sweet garden of Aphrodite,
to ascribe all cause to God
and love Karrhotos beyond all companions.

To the house of the swayed kings in the line of Battos
he led not by the hand late-thinking
Epimetheus' daughter, Excuse;
rather, beside Kastalia's
spring, a stranger, he laid on your hair the garland of the
  highest, for chariots.

With reins untangled
through the field of twelve fleet courses
he shattered no strength of his gear. The skilled
smith's intricate
work of hand he brought, passing
the hill of Krisa, is hung
in the God's hollow glade,
where the cypress-wood chamber
keeps it, next that image,
the tree's single growth, that the archer Kretans
dedicated to the king of Parnassos.

With glad heart it becomes you
now to greet him. He has done well.
Son of Alexibias, the fair-haired Graces flare about you.
Blessed are you, that even
after the huge toil
you have remembrance in mighty
words. Among forty
charioteers who fell, you brought
perfect your car through, and with heart unshaken,
and are come home from the shining of the games'
prizes to the plain of Libya and the city of your fathers.

No man is unallotted of labors, nor shall be;
but the prosperity from of old of Battos follows still, its course
  various,
tower of the city and eyes' shining
on strangers. Even deep-vaunting
lions fled him for fear

when he brought against them his speech of overseas.
And Apollo, leader of foundations,
gave the beasts over to flight and terror,
lest he be false in prophecy to the lord of Kyrene—

Apollo, who administers
to men and women healing of heavy sickness;
who gave the lyre and grants the Muse to whom he will,
bringing into their hearts
lawfulness without discord;
who sways the closed mantic
chamber. In which power at Lakedaimon,
in Argos and Pylos the sacrosanct
he has made dwell the strong sons
of Aigimios and of Herakles. Mine to sing
from Sparta the delight and the glory,

Sparta, whence begotten,
men of the stock of Aigeus came to Thera,
my fathers, not without gods, but a destiny led them.
Thereafter, Apollo Karneian,
in your festival, unfolding
contribution of much sacrifice,
we worship Kyrene's city
in its foundation of might;
city held also of strangers delighting in brazen warfare,
Trojans, Antenor's children, that came with Helen
when they had seen their own city smoking

in Ares. Men come now with gifts in their hands
and in due care propitiate with sacrifice a people of horses.
These are the men Aristoteles brought in fleet ships,
making open the deep ways of the salt water.
He founded the mightier groves of the gods,
and, with processionals to Apollo
that avert ills, he established
the paved street in the plain

to be trampled of horses; there at the edge of the market
place he lies apart in death.

Blessed he lived among men,
and therafter he is a hero the people worship.
And apart before his house are other holy
kings, who have death for their lot,
and with perception under the earth
hear great achievement
drenched in the delicate dew
of hymns outpoured: their own
wealth and the grace deserved and held in common
with Arkesilas, their son. And in choir of young men
it beseems him now to invoke Phoibos of the golden sword,

who holds from Pytho
the ransom for expense in splendor of victory,
song's grace. This man is praised of the wise.
I speak what men say.
He ministers a mind
that outruns his years;
speech also; for daring he is the eagle
of wide wings among birds;
in games, strength, like a wall;
among the Muses he goes lightfooted from birth;
he has approved himself a subtle charioteer.

To all splendors in his own land he has dared
the entrance; now God, favoring, makes perfect his power,
and hereafter, you blessed sons of Kronos,
may you grant him in action as in deliberation
such things to have; let no autumn storm-blast
of winds break the bloom.
The great mind of Zeus guides
the angel in men he loves.
I pray that at Olympia also he will give this honor into the
house of Battos.

PYTHIA 6

Listen! It is the field of Aphrodite
with the fluttering eyes or the Graces
we labor now. We approach the templed
centerstone of the thunderous earth.
There stands builded for the glory of Emmenos' children
and Akragas of the river, and for Xenokrates,
a treasure house of song
for victory at Pytho in Apollo's
glen, with its burden of gold.

Neither rain driven from afar on the storm,
not the merciless armies
of the crying cloud, no wind shall sweep it, caught
and stricken with the blown debris into the corners
of the sea. The front shines in the clear air,
Thrasyboulos, on your father announcing
for you and yours the pride
of a chariot victory in the folds of Krisa—
a tale to run on the lips of men.

You, keeping Victory erect beside your right hand,
bring home the meaning
of the things men say once on the mountain Chiron,
Philyra's son, urged on strong Peleiades
left in his care: *First of all gods, honor*
the deep-voiced lord of the lightning and thunderstroke,
Zeus Kronides;
next, through all their destiny never deprive
your parents of such reverence even as this.

In the old days mighty Antilochos proved one
who lived in that word.

74

He died for his father, standing up
to the murderous onset of the Aithiop champion,
Memnon; for Nestor's horse, smitten by the shaft of Paris,
had fouled the chariot, and Memnon attacked
with his tremendous spear.
And the old Messenian was shaken
at heart and cried aloud on his son's name.

And the word he flung faltered not to the ground; in that
    place
standing, the young man
in his splendor bought by his own death his father's rescue,
And of those who lived long ago men judged him
pre-eminent among the youth for devotion
to those who begot them, for that terrible deed.
All that is past.
Of men living now, Thrasyboulos
comes beyond others to the mark in his father's eyes,

and visits his father's brother with fame complete.
He carries wealth with discretion.
The blossom of youth he gathers is nothing violent,
but wise in the devious ways of the Muses.
To you, Poseidon, shaker of the earth, lord
of the mastering of horses, he comes, with mind to please
    you.
Also his heart, that is gentle
in the mixing of friends,
passes for sweetness the riddled work of the bees.

PYTHIA 7

The great city of Athens is the loveliest
invocation, to cast down as foundation stone for the song
to magnify the wide-flung strength of the sons of Alkmaion,
   and their victory with horses.
What country could you live in? what habitation? and name
one more conspicuous
for all Hellas to attend.

In every city the tale is an intimate thing
of the citizens of Erechtheus. At holy Pytho, Apollo,
they made magnificent the front of your templed house.
I am guided by five wins at the Isthmos, one pre-eminent
at Olympia, Zeus' own,
two victories gained from Kirrha—

yours, Megakles, and your fathers' before you.
In your late success I find some pleasure, but am troubled
at rancor changing beautiful things done. Even so, men say,
blessedness that remains
by a man to blossom over him brings,
with good, some things that are otherwise.

PYTHIA 8

Hesychia, kind goddess of peace, daughter
of Justice and lady of the greatness of cities:
you who hold the high keys
of wars and of councils,
accept for Aristomenes this train of Pythian victory.
For you understand, in strict measure of season,
deeds of gentleness and their experience likewise.

And you, when one fixes
anger without pity fast in his heart,
are stern to encounter
the strength of the hateful ones, and sink
pride in the bilge. Porphyrion understood you not
when wantonly he vexed you. Gain is sweet
if one carry it from the house of him who gives in good will.

But violence and high vaunting fail at the last.
Typhon the Kilikian, the hundred-headed, avoided not this,
nor yet the king of the Giants. They were smitten down by
    the thunderbolt
and the bow of Apollo, who now in mood of kindness
has received Xenarkes' son, home from Kirrha and garlanded
with leaves of Parnassos and with song in the Dorian strain.

This island, that in its city's
righteousness has touched
the famed valors of the Aiakidai, has not
fallen away from the Graces. She keeps
glory perfect from the beginning and is sung of many
for her shaping of heroes that surpassed in excellence
of games, and in the speed of their fighting also.

These things shine in her men likewise.
In my haste I cannot lay
leisure of long-drawn speech
on the lyre and the soft singing,
lest surfeit come to vex. Let your own need, my child,
and your youngest splendors run the path at my feet,
made a thing of speed by my fashioning.

For at wrestling you go the way of your mother's brethren,
nor shame Theognetos at Olympia,
nor Kleitomachos' victory of tough limbs at Isthmos.
Prospering the city of the Meidylidai, you wear the saying
Oikles' son spoke darkly once, as he watched
the young men enduring the spears in the seven gates of
  Thebes,

when the latter-born came again
to Argos, a second journey.
Thus he spoke, in their striving:
"The heritage of valor from their fathers shines
through in the sons' blood. I gaze in wonder and see plain
Alkmaon steering the spangled snake on his bright
shield, foremost in the gates of Kadmos.

"And he that flinched in that first disaster,
the hero Adrastos, now
goes compassed by message of augury
more favorable. Yet in his own house
otherwise shall he fare. Alone out of the Danaan host,
he shall gather the ashes of his son perished, and by the gods'
  chance
shall come home with the rest of his people scatheless

"to the wide streets of the city of Abas." Thus
the voice of Amphiaraos. And I also take joy
to cast a garland on Alkmaon and drench him in song.

He is my neighbor and the keeper of my possessions;
he met me in the way as I went to the singing centerstone of
    the earth,
and with the sooth that is his by blood made prophecy.

But you, archer of the far cast, lord
of the famed temple, where all gather,
in the deep folds of Pytho,
have granted this boy delight that is highest;
and, before now, a gift to fold in the arms,
you brought him home in triumph of your own five-contests.
My lord, I pray you that of my heart's will

I look on each thing in my course
even as you look also.
Justice herself stands over
the sweet singing in celebration; but I ask, Xenarkes,
the gods' gaze unresentful upon your fortunes.
For if one, even without long-drawn labors, compass splen-
    dors,
to many he seems as a wise man among fools

to crown his life with device and straight counsels.
Yet this lies not with men; God's luck is the giver,
that casts one man now aloft, and yet another beneath his
    hand.
Come back to measure. You have your prize at Megara,
and in the recess of Marathon; and with three successes,
Aristomenes, you have won at home the games of Hera.

And above four bodies you threw
your weight and your rage.
To these lads was ordained
at the Pythiad no delightful homefaring,
nor, as they came to their mothers, did laughter break sweetly
    about them

to stir delight. Down back ways, avoiding mockers,
they skulk, all stricken with their sad fortune.

But he that has won some new
splendor, in high pride
of hope rides the air
on the wings of his man's strength, and keeps
desire beyond his wealth. In brief space mortals'
delight is exalted, and thus again it drops to the ground,
shaken by a backward doom.

We are things of a day. What are we? What are we not? The
  shadow of a dream
is man, no more. But when the brightness comes, and God
  gives it,
there is a shining of light on men, and their life is sweet.
Aigina, dear mother, bring this city to haven
in free guise, by Zeus' aid and strong Aiakos',
Peleus and goodly Telamon aiding, and with Achilles.

PYTHIA 9

My desire, with the deep-girdled Graces aiding,
is to sing Telesikrates, proclaiming him
Pythian conqueror in the race with the brazen shield,
a blessed man and a garland upon Kyrene, mistress of char-
iots—
Kyrene that once from the windy folds of Pelion Lato's son
Apollo, he of the flowing hair,
carried away, a wild maiden, in his car of gold, to make her
dwell as queen in a country rich in flocks, in grain most rich,
flowering and desired, third branch of the mighty earth.

And Aphrodite, she whose feet are as silver, welcomed
her brother of Delos, laying a light hand
on the chariot built by skill of gods.
Over the delight of their bed she cast a spell of winsome shy-
ness,
joining the close union of the god lying with the daughter of
powerful Hypseus,
king in that time of the haughty Lapiths and a hero in the
second generation
from Ocean; whom on a time in the storied valleys of Pindos
a naiad nymph, Kreousa, brought to birth, after her joy with
Peneus;

Earth's daughter. And Hypseus reared a child,
Kyrene of the white arms. She loved not the shuttling ways
of the loom,
nor joy of circling dances in the house with the mates of her
age,
but with bronze-shod throwing-spears
and the sword's blade, she encountered and slew wild beasts,

81

bringing great quietness and peace upon
her father's herds; and little time she had for sleep, sweet
   night
companion, nor let it lie
long over her eyes at the breaking time of dawn.

Apollo, of the broad quiver and arrows that range
afar, saw her one day, wrestling alone,
unarmed, with a fell lion. Straightway,
lifting his voice, he called from his chamber of stone Chiron:
"Son of Philyra, leave your grave cavern to admire the
   strength of a girl
and her spirit also, the fight she carries cool-headed; a
   maiden with heart too high
for distress. Her bosom knows not the winter of fear.
What mortal could have begotten her? From what nurture
   torn

"keeps she the secret places of the shadowy hills?
Her valor is of that which has no ending.
Might it be becoming if I were to lay
my famed hand on her body, even cull the delicate meadows
   in her bed?"
And the centaur, prophetic, with a cool smile and a lift of
   his brow, made answer
straightway: "Secret are the keys kept of wise Persuasion to
   love's sacraments,
Phoibos; gods would blush and men likewise to enter
openly before all on the delight of love's first encounter.

"And you, whom lies are forbidden to touch,
some genial humor has stirred you to this irony. Whence the
   race of this girl
you ask, my lord? You know the appointed end
of each thing and the ways they are brought to pass;
and the number of the spring leaves earth blossoms, the
   number

of the sands in the sea and the rivers,
shaken by the waves and the streaming winds; and things to
  be
and whence they shall come to pass. All this you know.
But if I must match myself against your wisdom,

"I will speak: you have come to this glade
her bridegroom. You shall carry her over the sea
to the favored garden place of God.
There you shall make her queen of a city, assembling
a people of islanders to the ness between two plains; and
  Libya, lady of fair meadows,
shall welcome gladly in the golden house the bride in her
  glory. She shall be given
straightway and in full measure an allotment of earth
not without destiny of various growing things, nor unknown
  of beasts.

"There she will bear a son whom glorious Hermes,
lifting from the side of his beloved mother, will bring
to the Hours and Earth in their thrones of magnificence.
These, admiring in the brightness the child at their knees,
will minister to his lips ambrosia and nectar, and make him
  to be immortal,
a Zeus, a holy Apollo, a delight to men, beloved and trusty
  keeper of flocks,
to be called spirit of the wilds and the pastures, and to some
  Aristaios."
With these words he made ready the wedding's sweet
  accomplishment.

Rapid is the action of gods quickened
to move, and brief their ways. That day those things were
  done. In the golden chamber
of Libya they were brought together. There she sways
a city of loveliness and glory in contests.

Even now at Pytho the sacrosanct, Karneiades' son
has brought her close to the flowering of success;
by his victory he has made Kyrene shine afar, and she in
   kindness will welcome him
back to that city of lovely women,
bringing from Delphoi home the winsome glory.

High achievements run ever to many words,
but to elaborate few things among many
for the wise is to be heard. But Season in all things
keeps the utter heights. Thebes of the seven gates
upon a day knew Iolaos, how he failed not this. He severed
   Eurystheus'
head with the sword's edge, and they laid him under the
   earth at the tomb of the charioteer,
Amphitryon, his forefather, where he lay, guest-friend to the
   men of the dragon's teeth,
a dweller now in the city of the Kadmeians and the streets
   with white horses.

Joined to him and to Zeus, Alkmana
the wise in a single travail bore
the overmastering strength in battle of twin sons.
Stupid is the man, whoever he be, whose lips defend not
   Herakles,
who remembers not the waters of Dirke that gave him life,
   and Iphikles.
I, who have had some grace of them, shall accomplish my
   vow to bring them glory; let only the shining
light of the singing Graces fail me not. Ere now, I say that at
   Aigina
and beside the hill of Nisos three times I have sung the
   praise of this city,

escaping in proof the embarassment of silence.
Therefore, be a citizen friend or opponent, let him not darken
   the thing

labored well for the good of all, but keep the word of the
    sea's ancient,
who gave counsel to praise even the foeman
that with all his heart and in righteousness accomplishes fair
    things.
In the seasonable games of Pallas, Telesikrates, the maidens
    and women who saw you conquer prayed
voiceless and each aside that you might be
beloved husband or else as a son to them.

So also at the Olympian games, those
of Earth the deep-bosomed, and the games in the cities.
I, staunching the thirst of song,
am driven by some need once again to waken the memory,
ancient though it be, of your fathers: how they came for the
    sake of a Libyan woman
to Irasa city, suitors for Antaios' glorious daughter of the
    lovely hair.
Many were the princes among her kindred who sought her
hand, and many outlanders also. There was a splendor

of beauty upon her, and their will was to reap
the flowering pride of youth of the gold garlands that was
    hers.
Her father designed for his child a bridal to be famed
afar. He had heard how Danaos once in Argos
had caused his eight and forty daughters to be bestowed in
    marriage most fleet
before midday was sped; for he let the whole choir of them
    stand at the edge of the running field
and in competitions for speed of foot disposed
the maiden to be given each hero of all his sons-in-law.

Thus Antaios bestowed his daughter, finding her a Libyan
youth to wed. She was set at the mark in her glory, to be the
    prize,

and he spoke in their midst: that man should have her who
   in his driving pace
caught first at her robe's edge.
Alexidamos, run free of the straining pack,
took by the hand the grave maiden
and led her away through the multitude of the nomad riders.
   Many flowers
they heaped upon them, and garlands, even
as many were the wings of victory he had put on him in
   time before.

PYTHIA 10

Blessed is Lakedaimon,
happy Thessaly. Both have kings of one line
from Herakles, best in battle.
Is this boasting to no point? But Pytho and Pelinna lead me
on, and Aleuas' sons, to bring to Hippokleas
ringing praise of a chorus of men.

He has his share of prizes.
In the host of the dwellers-about, the crook of Parnassos
knew him best of boys in the double race.
Apollo, the end is made sweet and the beginning
for men when God drives; by your design he did it,
only he stepped in the tracks of his father,

Olympic winner twice in the warlike
armor of Ares,
and the games in the deep meadow under Kirrha's
rocks saw Phrikias best of sprinters.
May destiny, closing in later days,
make wealth blossom to glory about them.

Out of the joys in Hellas
let them take no small share, never encounter
the gods' thought shifting to evil. To be without grief
of heart is to be god; but blessed, worthy the poet's song, is
    the man
who by excellence of hand and speed in his feet
takes by strength and daring the highest of prizes,

living yet, sees his son
in the turn of his youth reaping Pythian garlands.

He cannot walk in the brazen sky, but among
those goods that we of mortality attain to he goes
the whole way. Never on foot or ship could you find
the marvelous road to the feast of the Hyperboreans.

Perseus came to them once, a leader of men,
entered their houses,
found them making hecatombs of asses
to Apollo, who in their joyance and favorable
speech rejoices, and smiles to see
the rampant lust of the lewd beasts.

Never the Muse is absent
from their ways: lyres clash, and the flutes cry,
and everywhere maiden choruses whirling.
They bind their hair in golden laurel and take their holiday.
Neither disease nor bitter old age is mixed
in their sacred blood; far from labor and battle

they live; they escape scandal
and litigation. Danaë's son came that day,
breathing strength in his heart, and Athene led him
to mix with those blessed men. He killed the Gorgon, came
bearing the head, intricate with the snake hair,
the stone death to the islanders. It is not mine

to wonder; when the gods appoint it,
nothing is too strange.
Check the oar now, grapple the anchor quick to the
beach at the prow, guard at the rock-reef.
See, the shimmering of the song's praise
skims as a bee does, story to story.

Now as the Ephyraians
shed my sweet song at the Peneios banks, I hope
even more to make with songs for the garlands' sake

Hippokleas honored among the youth and his elders,
and to young maidens a troubled thought, for, as
the age changes, new loves flutter the heart.

That which a man desires,
if he grasp, he must keep it in care beside him.
A year hence nothing is plain to see.
My trust is in the hospitality of Thorax; his favor, wafted,
yoked me this chariot of the Pierides,
friend to friend, leader to leader in kindness.

Gold shines gold when you test it
and the right wisdom.
Also I shall praise the noble brothers, because
they carry aloft the Thessalian way
and increase it. In their good hands is rested
the gift of their fathers, excellent government of cities.

Daughters of Kadmos, Semele, dweller among the Olympians,
and Ino, the white goddess,
keeper of the chambered sea among Nereus' daughters,
come in company of Herakles' mother
of high degree to Melia and the shrine that is treasure house of golden
tripods, honored beyond all else of Apollo,

who has named it Ismenian, true seat of prophecy.
Children of Harmonia, there
he summons you, a conclave of fiefed queens
to assemble together
and sing Themis, Pytho, and the earth's
center, where the decrees are strict, at the edge of evening:

a grace on Thebes of the seven
gates, and the contest at Kirrha,
where Thrasydaios woke the fame of the hearth
of his fathers, casting upon it a third garland,
victor in the abundant lands of Pylades
that was friend of old to Lakonian Orestes.

Him, as his father fell, cut down by Klytaimnestra's
strong hands, the nurse
Arsinoë snatched from the treacherous act of death,
even as the queen with stroke of gray bronze sent
Dardanian Priam's daughter,
Kassandra, to pass with Agamemnon's ghost to the shadowy strand of Acheron,

a pitiless lady. Was it Iphigeneia, who at the Euripos crossing
was slaughtered far from home,
that vexed her to drive in anger the hand of violence?
Or was it couching in a strange bed
by night that broke her will and set her awry—for young
    wives
a sin most vile, and that may not be hidden ever

from neighbors and their speech.
Fellow-citizens are fain to speak evil.
Grand wealth keeps envy to match its bulk,
while he who breathes low speaks and none hear.
Atreides, the hero, returning home in time delayed,
fell at Amyklai the glorious,

and brought to her death also the mantic maiden, after
he had broken from their delicacy of wealth the houses of
    Troy,
burned with fire for the sake of Helen. But Orestes, the young
    head of a kingdom,
came to his aged friend, Strophios,
at his home beside the foot of Parnassos; and with late-visited
    Ares
slew his mother, and laid Aigisthos low in his blood.

Friends, have I been whirled about at the shift of the cross-
    roads,
though I went the right way before?
Has some gale driven me from
my course, like a boat on the sea?
Muse, it rests with you, if for hire you have contracted me to
    render
my silvered voice, to stir one theme and another

for this man's father Pythonikos
and again for Thrasydaios.
The kindliness of glory burns as a light about them.

Long ago with chariots they were made beautiful with success.
At Olympia, and the games bespoken afar,
the running nimbus of victory in the horse race was theirs,

and now at Pytho they have come down into the naked course to deny
the assembled host of the Hellenes
by the speed in their feet. May God grant me love for that which has splendor;
but in this time of my life let me strive for attainable things;
for I have looked in the city and found the middle estate flowers
in prosperity far longer. I scorn the destiny of tyrants.

I am strung to the common virtues; the envious are put aside.
Of these if a man win the uttermost
and, shepherding it in peace, escape the blame
of pride, more beautiful is the ending he makes
in dark death, and to his sweet posterity
hands down the mightiest of possessions, grace of good name.

Such grace as makes glorious Iphikles'
son, Iolaos, a hero
of songs, and the great strength of Kastor,
and you, lord Polydeukes, twin sons of gods
who dwell by day in the founded earth of Therapne,
by night on Olympos.

Beloved brightness, loveliest of the cities of mortals,
house of Persephone, you who keep by the banks of Akragas
where the sheep wander, the templed hill—I beseech you,
   lady,
graciously, in the kindness of men and immortals likewise,
accept from Pytho this garland for splendid Midas;
accept him also. He has beaten Hellas at the art that once
Pallas Athene found when she followed in song
the death dirge of the bitter Gorgons.

She heard that melody in the agony of their sorrow, dripping
down from the forbidding, snake-locked heads of the
   maidens,
after Perseus slew one of the three sisters
and brought home death to the people in Seriphos by the sea.
Surely he blinded the strange race of Phorkos
and made a bitterness of the feast of Polydektes, and his
   mother's
long slavery and her bed of necessity,
by drawing forth the head of lovely Medusa,

he, Danaë's son, who, I affirm, was born of the raining gold.
The maiden goddess, when she had saved her friend
from distress, discovered the polyphonal music of flutes,
with instruments to mimic the wailing clamor
that grew from the mouthing jaws of Euryala.
The goddess found it and, finding, gave it to mortals to use,
naming it the melody many-headed,
splendid herald of rivalries to rouse people,

rippling forth from the thin bronze bound on reeds
that dwell next to the Graces' city of lovely meadows
in the holy domain of Kephisos, fair witnesses to the dancers.
Success for men, if it comes ever, comes not unattended
with difficulty. A god can end it, even
today. That which is fated you cannot escape. But a time
  will come
such that it will strike in amazement beyond
expectation, to give one thing desired, to withhold another.

NEMEA 1

Grave child of the waters of Alpheos,
leafed branch of glorious Syracuse, Ortygia,
resting place of Artemis,
sister of Delos, from you the sweetly spoken
hymn begins, to shape
the great strain of praise for horses with storm in their feet,
   by grace of Zeus on Aitna;
and the chariot of Chromios is urgent with me, and Nemea,
   to link the song of glory for triumph in contests.

The beginnings are cast down by the gods,
aided by that man's divine gifts.
The uttermost of reputation lies
in achievement; for high trials
the Muse would be remembered in singing.
Scatter, now, some glory on this island, that the lord of
   Olympos,
Zeus, gave Persephone, and bowed his head to assent, the
   pride of the blossoming earth,

Sicily, the rich, to control under towering cities
opulent;
Kronion granted her also
a people eager in brazen warfare,
horsemen; a people garlanded over and again with the
   golden leaves of olive
Olympian. I mount this occasion
for manifold praise, nor cast my words in falsehood.

I stand at the courtyard gates
of a generous host and lead the lovely song.

There the delight of the feast
is ordered to splendor, the house knows well
guests that throng from afar.
It is the privilege of great men to quench the smoke of envy
against traducers. Skills vary with the man. We must tread a
   straight path and strive by that which is born in us;

for strength is realized in action,
and mind in council, predicting the way to come
of inborn nature.
Son of Agesidamos, in the way of your nature lies
that which will achieve all manner of things.
I love not vast wealth darkened deep in the house,
but with it there to know good treatment and reputation; to
   serve friends. The hopes of men that labor long

have some community. I give you now
with glad heart
Herakles, great in the high places
of valor. I raise again an ancient story
how, when that child of Zeus escaped the darkness of labor
   and came
with his twin brother forth
from his mother's loins into the brightness,

he came not unmarked by Hera
of the golden throne, even in his child's wrappings saffron
   dyed;
but the queen of the gods
in her heart's anger sent two snakes upon him straightway.
These came through the opened gates
into the great inner chamber, raging to grip the children
in their swift jaws. But Herakles raised his head upright and
   tasted his first battle,

with two unescapable hands,
clutching the throat of either serpent,

96

locked to crush
the strangling breath from their terrible bodies.
But fear beyond endurance
smote the women that tended Alkmana's lying-in,
and she herself, barefooted as she was, sprang from the bed
   to fight the rearing monsters.

And with speed the lords of the Kadmeians, assembled
in armor
of bronze, ran in; and Amphitryon,
shaking in his hand the sword torn from its sheath,
came stricken with savage doubt. That which is close to
   home afflicts all alike,
but a heart soon goes free of grief
over a stranger's unhappiness.

He stood in painful amazement mixed
with joy, for he saw the unnatural
courage and strength of his son.
The gods had ordained the upshot to contradict
his messengers.
But he called on his neighbor, the great prophet of Zeus on
   high,
Teiresias, the strict seer; who told before him and all the
   company his son's encounters to be,

all the beasts he must slay by land,
all the beasts of the sea, brutes without right or wrong;
likewise the man walking, crossed
with conceit in hatefulness,
he must give over to death;
and how, when the gods in the plain of Phlegra met the
   Giants in battle,
under the storm of his shafts these also must drag their bright
   hair in the dust.

All this he told; and in time how Herakles should have the
    rest
of eternity in peace,
in quittance of great things done;
rest and a life beyond all men
in the blessed house, and with blossoming Hebe given to be
    his wife, and domain;
and, feasting beside Kronian Zeus,
should praise the high design of the gods.

NEMEA 2

Even as the Homeridai,
the rhapsode singers of stories, for the greater part
begin with a prelude to Zeus, so this man also
is given his first choral for victory in the sacred games at
    Nemea
in Zeus' grove, the much-besung.

If his life in its speed
along the path his fathers trod has given
glory to great Athens, it is his due
over and again to reap the splendid flowers of Isthmian vic-
    tories, Pythian also,
this son of Timonoös. It is fitting

for Orion to follow
not far behind the mountain Peleiades.
Likewise Salamis is strong to build a man who can be
a fighter. At Troy, Hektor gave way before Ares. O Timo-
    damos, your strength
and patient courage in the pankration will bring you
    through.

Acharnai's sons (it is proverbial)
are brave men, and for contests
the Timodamidai are pre-eminent in men's speech.
From beside high, brooding Parnassos they brought home
    four victories in the games;
and at the hands of the men of Korinth

in the hollows of princely Pelops
they have gathered into their arms ere now eight garlands,
seven at Zeus' festival in Nemea, at home
time beyond number. Citizens, make Zeus your song as
    Timodamos comes home in triumph.
Strike up the sweet choral singing.

99

NEMEA 3

Lady and Muse, our mother, I entreat you,
in the holy Nemean month, come to the city thronged with
    strangers,
the Dorian island, Aigina; for beside
the waters of Asopos the craftsmen of lovely
choral songs, the young men, await your voice.
Every achievement has a different thirst,
but victory in games longs beyond all for singing
and the skill to glorify garlands and strength proved.

Of such inspiration grant me abundance.
Daughter to the cloudy king of the sky, begin
his stately song. And I shall elaborate it
with voice and in the lyre's strain. Gracious will be the work
of glorification of the land where the Myrmidons lived
in old time, whose legendary assembling place
Aristokleides, under your destiny, lady, stained not
with reproach, weakening under the circling strength

of contestants in the pankration. To heal
the painful blows taken in the deep Nemean plain, he brings
    home the splendor of victory.
Beautiful as he is and with work not shaming his stature,
this son of Aristophanes has come to the uttermost manliness.
    So. Further
you cannot go lightly in the impassable sea, beyond the pil-
    lars of Herakles,

which the heroic god set down, to mark in fame
journey's end. He broke monsters that rose
up out of the sea, tested the current of every
shoal, to where the end was and the turning-point for home.

100

He explored the land. My heart, to what alien headland
do you fetch my course along shore?
I say we must bring music to Aiakos and his race.
For highest justice attends the saying: *Praise the good.*

Passions for things alien are not best for a man to have.
Seek nearer home. You have found glory that lends occasion
for fair speech. Among men of old, Peleus
rejoiced in valor, who cut the spear that surpassed all others,
who took Iolkos alone, with no host behind him,
who caught Thetis of the sea in his grasp.
And Telamon of the vast strength
stood by Iolaos to sack Laomedon's city,

and went with him against the Amazons strong in their
    brazen bows,
and the terror that breaks men did not stop the force in his
    heart.
The splendor running in the blood has much weight.
A man can learn and yet see darkly, blow one way, then
    another, walking ever
on uncertain feet, his mind unfinished and fed with scraps
    of a thousand virtues.

But tawny Achilles lived in the house of Philyra
and as yet a boy did great things; in his hands hefting
javelins scantly tipped with iron, wind-light,
he wreaked death in bloody combat upon wild lions;
he struck down boars, and to the house of the Kronian
centaur dragged the gasping carcasses,
at six years, and thereafter for the rest of his time;
and amazed Artemis and stern Athene,

killing deer without hounds or treacherous nets,
for he ran them down in his speed. I tell these tales
out of old time. Under his stone-caverned roof, Chiron

trained Jason, the deeply wise, and thereafter Asklepios,
teaching the gentle-handed way of healing.
He brought to pass the marriage
of Nereus' daughter of the shining breasts, and nursed
her magnificent son, waxing his heart to all things becoming,

so that, carried on the run of the sea winds, beneath Troy
he might stand up against the clamor and shock of spears of
    Lykians, Phrygians,
Dardanians, and come to handstrokes with hard-fighting
Aithiopians; and fix it in his heart that never more might
    come home
their lord, Helenos' valiant kinsman, Memnon.

Thence the shining of the Aiakidai has cast its light afar.
Their blood, Zeus, is yours, and yours the victory that the
    song peals out
in the voices of young singers, a delight for men that live
    near.
Their music shines forth with Aristokleides also,
who has brought this island again into men's speech of
    praise,
and likewise by his splendid ambitions the Thearion
of the Pythian god. The end shines through
in the testing of actions where excellence is shown,

as a boy among boys, a man among men, last
among the elders, each part that makes
our mortal life. Human destiny drives
four excellences, with urgency to think of the thing at hand.
This fails not here. Hail, friend. I send you this,
mixed of pale honey
and milk, and a liquid shining is on the mixture,
a draught of song rippled in Aiolian flutes,

late though it come. Among birds the eagle is swift.
Pondering his prey from afar, he plummets suddenly to blood
the spoil in his claws.
Clamorous daws range the low spaces of the sky.
Aristokleides, by grace of Kleo throned on high, and your
own will to victory,
from Nemea and Epidauros, from Megara also, the light has
brightened about you.

NEMEA 4

The best healer for struggles of pain, after the issue is clear,
is happiness; and wise songs,
daughters of the Muses, stroke one with hands of gentleness.
Not warm water even laps in such ease
the body as praise molded to the lyre's measure.
The story of things done outlives the act
when, by the Graces' assent,
the lips lift it up out of the deep heart.

Let this be the proem of the hymn I cast
for Zeus, child of Kronos, for Nemea
and Timasarchos' wrestling; may it find favor in
the established tower of the Aiakidai, light of fair salvation
  to all
strangers. And if Timokritos, your father, still went warm
in the sun's blaze, over and again with intricacy
of lyre playing, leaning upon this melody,
he would have chanted the splendor of his son's success;

the chain of garlands from the games at Kleonai
brought home; and from shining
Athens the magnificent; at Thebes of the seven gates,
where beside the bright tomb of Amphitryon
the Kadmeians with good will circled him with flowers
for Aigina's sake. Friend among friends, he came
to the city of his hosts, to look
upon the rich court of Herakles,

with whom mighty Telamon long ago sacked
Troy, slew the Meropes
and the armed ghastly giant Alkyones—

not before he had crushed with the boulder twelve
chariots and twice as many heroes, tamers of horses,
that rode them. The man who understands not
this, understands not fighting; nothing
is accomplished without loss to the man who does it.

I am barred from telling these things by the song's rule
and time insistent upon me,
yet I am dragged by a new-moon magic to lay my hands
    thereon.
Still, though the deep sea's water lie
between, resist conspiracy; thus shall we show
far better than our enemies, and come down to the trial in
    brightness.
A man looking upon another in envy
drives the vain shaft of his opinion in darkness, wavering,

to drop groundward. Such virtue as lordly
Destiny has bestowed on me,
I know time surging shall bring it to the fulness ordained.
Now, my sweet lyre, weave out
in Lydian harmony a song beloved
of Oinona and Kypros, where Telamonian Teukros
is given his lordship. Aias
keeps Salamis, after his father's right.

And in the Euxine sea Achilles has his bright
island. Thetis is queen
in Phthia. Neoptolemos sways the Mainland at the strait,
where the grazed headlands sprawl, running
all the way down from Dodona to the Ionian crossing.
Beside the foot of Pelion, turning
against Iolkos the hand of violence, Peleus gave it
over to slavery, and to the men of Haimonia to be theirs.

He had endured the treachery of Akastos' wife,
Hippolyta, and her lewd designs.

Her lord, Pelias' son, planned death for her sake by ambush
and the fair-wrought knife; but Chiron stood by Peleus,
and the destiny of Zeus' design brought him through.
When he had withstood the overwhelming force of fire, the
    savagery
of lions, the stroke of the tearing
claws, the ghastly teeth,

he married one of the throned Nereids of the deep.
He saw in a grand circle the sessions
of the sky's kings and the kings of the sea beside him,
the gifts they gave and the power for his race thereafter.
Into the night beyond Gades you may not pass; bend back
against the shore of Europe your ship's gear.
There are no means for me
to tell all the long tale of the sons of Aiakos.

But I have come to the Theandridai a glad herald
of games in their strength,
and I unite them with Olympia, with Nemea and the Isthmos.
They tried their strength there and came home
not without garlands in their famed leafage, so that we all
    may know,
Timasarchos, how your country is minister
to hymns of victory. If you bid
that I raise up also to Kallikles, your uncle,

a monolith shining whiter than Parian stone:
gold tested in the heat
shows forth the full blaze of its glory, and the song
of brave things done makes a man's fortune rival
kings. Let him, who dwells now beside Acheron,
hear yet my voice's cry, where in the contest
of the trident wielder, Poseidon the deep-thundering,
he was glorified with the parsley wreath of Korinth.

Euphanes, your aged forefather, would have sung gladly
in his honor, before their kinsmen;
and others, fellows of an age, before others; a man's hope is
to bespeak what he has seen himself beyond all beside.
Let one so praising Melesias parry bitterness,
grappling the words, one not to be overthrown by sleight of
  speech,
one whose thoughts toward the right men are kindly,
but who will second him fiercely against his enemies.

I am no maker of images, not one to fashion idols standing
    quiet
on pedestals. Take ship of burden rather, or boat, delight of
    my song,
forth from Aigina, scattering the news
that Lampon's son, Pytheas the strong,
has won the garland of success at Nemea, pankratiast,
showing not yet on his cheeks the summer
of life to bring soft blossoming.

He has done honor to the fighting heroes descended of Zeus
    and Kronos, and the golden
Nereids, the Aiakidai; he has honored the city his mother, a
    land beloved of strangers
that once they prayed might be famous for ships and for men,
standing before the altar of their father, Zeus Hellanios,
and spread their arms in the air
together, the renowned sons of Endais,
with the man of great strength, Phokos

the goddess' son, that Psamatheia
brought forth on the beach where the sea breaks.
I take shame to speak of a thing done
monstrous, adventured against justice,
how they left their island of fair fame,
how some god drove
these mighty men from Oinona. I stop there. Not every sheer
    truth
is the better for showing her face. Silence also
many times is the wisest thing for a man to have in his mind.

But if it is prosperity, or strength of hand, or the iron of war
   we must praise, let them
dig me a long pit for leaping. The spring in my knees is light.
The beating wings of eagles carry them over the sea.
On Pelion was sung before these generously the song
from the Muses' splendid choir, and among them
Apollo, stroking the seven strings
of his lyre with the golden plectrum,

was leader of the changing melody. The song in the begin-
   ning was Zeus; they sang of proud Thetis
and Peleus; how Kretheus' daughter, Hippolyta the luxu-
   rious, sought to ensnare him
by craft, beguiling her lord, king
of the Magnesians, by the subtlety of her designs.
She fabricated a story that was a lie,
how Peleus had sought to be with
her, a wife, in the bridal bed of Akastos.

It was the other way.
Over and again with all her heart
she had entreated him with her persuasions.
Indeed, the abrupt words had troubled his passion;
but he denied the girl forthwith,
fearing the anger of our Father
the Hospitable. And Zeus, who ranges the clouds, king of
   the immortals, was pleased
and from the sky bent his head to will that without delay
some Nereid of the sea, one of those who work with a golden
   spindle, should be his wife,

prevailing upon her kinsman, Poseidon, who many times
   fares over the sea from Aigai
to the great Dorian Isthmos, where the glad companies meet
   the god with a clamor of reed flutes
and dare the strength of their limbs in contest.

Destiny in the blood decides all
action. Euthymenes, twice at Aigina you
were folded into the arms of victory
and given formal glorification in song.

Now again, Pytheas, your uncle's pride is in your feet that
    go in the track of his blood.
Nemea was his and the month in the land Delphinios, Apol-
    lo's beloved.
You at home defeated all comers of your age
and at the fair curve of the hill of Nisos. All your city
is a contender in lordly deeds, and I am glad.
Know that in success you have repaid
delight to Menandros, your trainer, for hard work

given. (A smith to mold
athletes must come from the city of Athens.)
If, my song, you adventure
into the presence of Themistios, fear not.
Speak out, run the sails aloft
to the crossbar at the masthead.
Speak of him as pankratiast and boxer, who achieved at
    Epidauros
twofold success, and now before the doors of Aiakos
wears the wreath luxuriant with flowers, the gift of the fair-
    haired Graces.

NEMEA 6

There is one
race of men, one race of gods; both have breath
of life from a single mother. But sundered power
holds us divided, so that the one is nothing, while for the
  other the brazen sky is established
their sure citadel forever. Yet we have some likeness in great
intelligence, or strength, to the immortals,
though we know not what the day will bring, what course
after nightfall
destiny has written that we must run to the end.

For witness
even now, behold how his lineage works in Alkimidas.
It is like cornfields that exchange their estate,
now in their year to yield life to men from their level spaces
while again they lie fallow to gather strength. He came
home from the lovely games at Nemea,
a boy contestant; and steering this destiny from God
he shows now
as one not ill-starred in his quest of prizes for wrestling,

laying his feet in the steps that are his by blood
of his grandfather, Praxidamas.
He was Olympionician and first
brought home to the Aiakidai from Alpheus the olive
  branches,
and went five times garlanded at the Isthmos,
thrice at Nemea, to abate forgetfulness
fallen upon Sokleidas, mightiest
of the sons of Hagesimachos.

111

For these three
have come home, bearing prizes; their achievement reached
the uttermost;
and it was these who knew the struggle also. By God's grace,
boxing has brought forth no one house to possess
more garlands in any corner of all Hellas. I hope,
high though my speech be, it strikes the mark squarely,
as from a bow drawn true. My Muse, steer me the flight
of these my words
straight and glorious. For men pass,

but the songs
and the stories bring back the splendor of their deeds.
And the Bassidai have no dearth, their race is bespoken of
old,
as on long voyages they have come with a freight of praise,
for the gardeners of the Muses
giving occasion to hymns for the sake of high deeds.
Kallias also, of the blood of this same stock,
at sacred Pytho, his hands bound in the thongs,
won victory
and pleased the children of Lato of the gold hair,

and beside Kastalia at nightfall
was brightened in acclamation of the Graces.
The tireless bridge of the sea, at the two-year games
of the dwellers-about, where an ox is slaughtered,
glorified him in Poseidon's precinct.
And on a time the Lion's parsley
shaded his victor's brows in the dark glen
of Phleious under the primeval mountains.

Wide are the ways
from all sides, for the tellers of tales
to glorify this splendid island; for the Aiakidai
have made mighty its destiny, showing forth great things
done in valor,

and over the earth and across the seas afar wings
the name of them; as far as the Aithiopians
it went suddenly when Memnon came not home. Heavy
was the assault of Achilles
when he came down from his chariot

and with the
edge of the angry sword struck down the child
of the shining Dawn. All this is a way the men
before me discovered long ago, but I follow it also, carefully.
When the ship is laboring, always the wave that rolls nearest
    her forefoot,
they say, brings terror beyond aught else to all men's
hearts. But I gladly have taken on my back a twofold burden
and come a messenger,
heralding this twenty-fifth

triumph won from games that are called sacred.
Alkimidas, you have been true
to the splendor of your race. Twice, my child, at the precinct
of Kronian Zeus, only a random draw
despoiled you and Polytimidas of Olympian garlands.
Melesias I would liken
to a dolphin in his speed through the sea's water,
a man to guide the strength in a boy's hands.

Eleithyia, seated beside the grave, wise Muses,
child of almighty Hera, bringer of children to birth, listen:
   without you
we look not on daylight nor on black evening, receive not
for our own your sister of the young glorious limbs, Hebe.
The breath of life that all draw is not the same;
one thing or another tied to a destiny checks it. By your
   means
the son also of Thearion, Sogenes, predominant
for prowess, is made glorious in song for the five-contests.

He lives in the city that loves singing, city of the Aiakidai
of the crashing spears; with favor they guide a spirit like
   theirs, hardy in the struggle.
If a man be fortunate and win, he casts the delight
of his cause in the Muses' stream; even high strength,
lacking song, goes down into the great darkness.
There are means to but one glass that mirrors deeds of
   splendor;
by the shining waters of Memory
is found recompense for strain in poetry that rings far.

Wise men have learned of the third day's wind to come;
their greed does not bemuse them.
Rich man and poor move side by side toward the limit
of death. I think the tale
of Odysseus is greater than his deeds, all through the grace of
   Homer.

Upon his lies and the winged intelligence
there is a kind of majesty; genius persuasive in speech de-
   ceives us; blind

is the heart in the multitude of men. Else,
could they have seen the truth, never would great Aias,
angered over the weapons, have driven the burnished
sword through his own heart—after Achilles the strongest
   fighter
the west wind, straightening, carried in the swift ships
to bring back fair-haired Menelaos' lady

from Ilion. The wave of death comes over us all.
It breaks unexpected; it comes if you look for it also. Fame
   is theirs
for whom God makes delicate the legend after their death.
Beside the great, deep-folded navel
of the earth, there came as a helper he who lies
in the Pythian precinct, Neoptolemos, sacker of Priam's city,
where the Danaans labored long. On the home voyage
he lost Skyros, was driven and came to Ephyra.

A short while he was king
in Molossia; his seed carries that right
forever. He came to Apollo,
bringing gifts out of the spoil from Troy.
There, in a quarrel over the meats, a man with a knife
   stabbed him.

The hospitable Delphians were exceedingly heavy at heart.
But he gave destiny its own. It was fated that in the primeval
   grove
some one of the great Aiakidai must lie for the rest of time
beside the God's walled house, and with heroic processionals
dwell there, mantic, amid much sacrifice.
To make justice fair, three words will serve.
A witness who shall not lie stands over the things done,
Aigina, by your children and Zeus'. I am bold to speak

from within, by the high road of speech, over shining
excellence. But in all things rest is sweet; there is surfeit

even in honey, even in Aphrodite's lovely flowers.
By birth each of us is given his own life to carry.
They differ one way and another. No one man
can lift and hold blessedness entire; I cannot
speak of any to whom Destiny gave good, lasting
unshaken. Thearion, to you she proffers deserved occasion

for success; you dare splendid things,
and she does not make void the thoughtfulness in your heart.
I am a friend; I put aside the darkness of blame
and bring to a man beloved, like streams of water,
glory in sincere praise; such recompense befalls the good
     men.

An Achaian standing beside me will find no fault,
one who dwells beyond the Ionian sea. I trust in my proxeny.
     Among fellow-citizens
I look with clear eyes, without excess.
I keep my feet from all things violent; may time to come
be gracious accordingly. Let a man think, then say
if I go out of key, if my words are crooked.
Sogenes, descended of Euxenos, I swear
I have not overstepped the line, to cast my speech

in speed, like that bronze-shod javelin that released from the
     sweat
of wrestling the strength of your shoulders, without the sun's
     blaze on your body.
For what hard work there was, the joy that follows is greater.
Let be. If for the victor's sake I have raised
my voice too high, I am not too stubborn to set it aright.
Lightly will I make garlands. Strike up now. For you the
     Muse
binds gold upon white ivory with
the lily growth, raised dripping from the sea.

Mindful of Zeus, over Nemea
let the mixed clamor of the choral sound forth
in peace. It beseems us, in this dancing place,
to make our song's theme the king of the gods
in mild voice. They say he engendered Aiakos in the womb
   of his mother

to be lord of his own famous country
and, Herakles, your trusted guest-friend and brother. Of the
   good things given
between man and man, I say that a neighbor,
true and loving in heart, to neighbor is a joy beyond
all things else. If God sustain this,
grant, you who beat down the Giants, that Sogenes wish to
   dwell
in your favor beside his father, with gentle spirit toward him,
in the holy street fair-founded of his ancestors;

for, as in the cross-yoke of a four-horse chariot,
his house is between your precincts on either hand as you go.
   O Blessed,
yours it is to persuade Hera's lord
and the gray-eyed maiden. You can give men strength
over and again against bewilderment and distress.
As you made his life strong in body,
may you keep him thus in his shining youth and old age also
and make him fortunate; and his children's children

shall be given such favor and even more hereafter.
For me: my heart will not confess
I assaulted Neoptolemos in disorderly
words. To say this thrice and four times over
turns into futility, like the meaningless cry of children,
   Zeus Korinthos.

NEMEA 8

Divine Youth, messenger of Aphrodite
and her shining and immortal tendernesses,
you who lie on the eyelids of young girls, and of boys,
some you lift up with soft hands of necessity, others in
harder fashion.
It is a glad thing not to fail opportunity, and come in time
to each thing done, possessing those loves that are stronger.

Such were they who dispensed
the gifts of Kypris and tended the bed of Zeus
and Aigina. And from Oinona grew a son and a king,
splendid in council and the hand's work. And many over
and again entreated his presence,
for without advertisement the best of the heroes that dwelt
about him
asked, with no constraint, to obey his lordship,

they who at Athens of the rocks were the marshals of armies,
and the children of Pelops at Sparta.
For the sake of a beloved city and these its citizens
I embrace, in supplication, the hallowed knees of Aiakos,
bearing
this Lydian veil embroidered with clashing song,
a thing to glorify Deinias for his two-length race at Nemea,
and for Megas his father.
Success abides longer among men
when it is planted by the hand of God;

God who loaded Kinyras with weight of wealth
in sea-borne Kypros long ago.
I stand on light feet and draw my breath before I speak.

118

Many things have been spoken in many a way, but when one
   discovers a new thing and tests it
at the touchstone, there all is danger; talking delights the
   envious,
ever busy against the noble, meddling not with smaller men.

It was this that slaughtered the son of Telamon
and bent him over his own sword.
A quiet man, no talker, steadfast of heart, lies forgotten
in the rage of dispute. The great prize is given to the supple
   liar.
In their secret ballots the Danaans made much of Odysseus,
and Aias lost the golden armor and died struggling in his
   own blood.

In truth, otherwise were the gashes that in the onset
they tore in the warm flesh of their adversaries
under the spears of defense about Achilles' body,
in many another combat of those wasting
days. But hate, even then, was there with its pretexts.
It walks companion of beguiling words; it is sly and a spite
   that makes evil;
it violates the beautiful and brilliant
to lift up out of things obscure a glory rotten at the heart.

Zeus father, may such never be my way;
let me, walking always in the path
of simplicity, make my life, and die thus, leaving
to my children fame without reproach. Some pray for gold,
   some for lands
without limit, but I to lay my limbs in the ground as one who
   gladdened his fellow-citizens,
praising that which deserves it, scattering blame on the
   workers of evil.

But excellence waxes as the vine
growth in the young green tendrils,

raised up among the men who are righteous and wise into the
limpid sky. Various are the uses of friends, beyond all else
in difficulty, but joy also looks for trust that is clear
in the eyes. O Megas, bring back your soul to life,

I cannot; the end of empty hopes is despair;
but blithe am I to raise up to your city
and the Chariadai a marble column of the Muses because of
   the speed in your feet,
yours and your son's. I am glad to utter
a vaunt to match the very achievement; while by song a man
can take the pain even from labor. There were hymns of
   congratulation
long ago, before
the strife of Adrastos and the Kadmeians.

NEMEA 9

From Apollo and Sikyon, Muses, bring we the festival song
to new-founded Aitna, where the doors unfolded are
  thronged beyond their measure with guests,
and the rich house of Chromios; now make lovely the strain
  of song.
For, riding the chariot in its power of horses, he calls aloud
  to the mother and her twin children,
coholders and guardian divinities of the steep of Pytho.

There is a saying among men: *Hide not in grounded silence
a noble thing fulfilled*. Song in magic of words brings glorifi-
  cation.
Strike up, then, the thrum of the lyre, lift up the flute's cry
to crown the contest of horses Adrastos established for
  Phoibos beside Asopos' streams; and, remembering,
I will work out for that hero praise that shall ring far.

Then he was king in that place and with new festivals
and with contests of men's strength and with graven chariots
  showed forth his city's glory.
There was a time he fled the angry spirit of Amphiaraos and
  dread faction,
from the house of his fathers and Argos. Talaos' children,
  overborne in conflict, no longer were lords.
A stronger man beats down the right of old.

Eriphyle the baneful, as if to seal the oath,
they gave Oikles' son to wife. Thereafter they were the high
  lords of the fair-haired Danaans;
and on a day they led to seven-gated Thebes an army of men

not in the way of good augury; nor did Kronian Zeus, shak-
ing his thunderbolt against their insolence,
bid them go from home, but rather spare the venture.

But this throng hastened into destruction that showed plain
with brazen armor and horses and gear; and by Ismene's
banks, bereft
of sweet homecoming, they made rich with their bodies the
pale-blossoming smoke.
Seven corpse-fires fed on the young limbs of men; but Zeus
in all his strength, with lightning
split the deep-bosomed earth for Amphiaraos and covered
him and his horses,

or ever, stabbed in the back with Periklymenos' spear, that
warrior
shamed his own valor. In more than mortal panics even the
gods' sons flee.
O Kronion, if I may, I would put off to the utmost the
glorious trial
of spears for life and death with the Punic men; I ask you to
grant
to the sons of the Aitnaians that their destiny of fair laws
may abide long,

Zeus father, and that you bring this people to glory in their
city's domain.
Behold, these men love horses, and they have souls greater
than their possessions.
I speak, and none will believe; for honor, who brings glory,
is covered in secrecy
by love for gain. Carrying the shield for Chromios among
the foot and the horsemen and in the sea-fighting,
you had honored him amid the danger of the loud onset.

There in battle that goddess made strong his fighting heart
to beat off the blight of Ares. Few can take counsel

and turn aside the cloud of instant slaughter against the
    enemy ranks
with heart and hand; yet it is said that glory blossomed for
    Hektor beside Skamandros waters,
and by the deep-slung headlands of Eloros, where men

speak of Rhea's crossing, this same light
looked down on the son of Agesidamos in his first youth;
    and on other days
I might speak of much more done on the dusty land and the
    sea hard by.
But out of labors, for them who have with their youth
    righteousness, the day of their life grows green toward old
    age.
Let him know that at God's hand he is given prosperity to
    be admired.

For if with much possession a man win conspicuous honor,
there lies beyond no mark for a mortal to overtake with his
    feet.
But peace loves the gay banquet, and victory in its young
    growth prospers
with gentle song; and the voice becomes confident by the
    mixing-bowl.
Let them pour the wine, sweet prophet of revelry,

and serve the vine's strong child in the silver cups
his horses won for Chromios once and brought home with
    fairly plaited
wreaths of Apollo from holy Sikyon. Zeus father,
I pray that with the Graces' aid I may sing his excellence and
    on many occasions
honor success, throwing my spear right close to the Muses'
    mark.

NEMEA 10

Sing, O Graces, the city of Danaos and his fifty daughters of
  the shining
thrones, Argos, the house of Hera, fit dwelling place for
  gods. The flame of excellence
for brave things done in their thousands shines about it.
Long is the tale of Perseus and the Gorgon Medusa;
many are the cities of Egypt founded at Epaphos' hands;
there is Hypermestra the steadfast, who alone kept the
  sword's doom fast in its sheath.

And of old the gray-eyed maiden of the fair hair made
  Diomedes a god immortal;
at Thebes the earth, thunder-smitten by the bolts of Zeus,
  received
the seer, Oikles' son, storm-cloud of battle.
The city from of old surpasses in lovely-haired women;
a tale proved, for Zeus came to Alkmana and Danaë;
and for Adrastos' father and for Lynkeus he married the
  yield of their minds to straight justice.

He fostered the spear's might of Amphitryon, who, high in
  blessedness,
came even into his kinship, when in brazen armor
he slew the Teleboans, and in his likeness
the king of the immortals entered his courtyard,
carrying the fearless seed of Herakles, to whom on Olympos
Hebe is wife, loveliest of the goddesses, who walks beside
  her mother, lady of marriage.

My lips are brief to rehearse all that destiny of glories the
  holy ground
of Argos keeps. There remains surfeit of men, a harsh thing
  to encounter.

124

Nevertheless, wake the well-strung lyre
and take thought of wrestling now; for the brazen games
stir the people toward the ox-sacrifice of Hera, and the judg-
  ment of contests,
where Oulias' son, Theaios, twice has conquered to win for-
  getfulness of his labors lightly borne.

He has defeated the assembled Hellenes at Pytho and, com-
  ing with good fortune,
won the wreath at Nemea and the Isthmos, that the Muses
  be not idle;
and thrice at the Sea Gates success was his,
and thrice in the holy fields of Adrastos' domain.
Zeus father, his mouth is silent of his heart's desire; yet every
  end
of achievement lies in you. With heart not strange to en-
  deavor, he brings hardihood to beg grace.

I sing that which is known to God and all who strive
on the heights for the uttermost prizes. Pisa keeps
Herakles' ordinances supreme; yet twice before
in their ceremonies the Athenian voices have risen in sweet-
  ness
to acclaim him; and in earth burnt by fire and the keeping
  of figured vessels
the olive's yield has come to Hera's land of brave men.

Theaios, honor of games' success, with the Graces and the
  Tyndaridai,
attends always the seed renowned of your mother's people.
Were I kinsman of Thrasyklos and of Antias,
I would not deign in Argos to veil the light
of my eyes, for all the victories won, wherein Proitos' city of
  horses
has blossomed. In the recesses of Korinth and at the hands of
  the men of Kleonai they won four times.

From Sikyon they departed with silver of the wine goblets,
and from Pellana, mantling their shoulders in robes soft
woven.
But the thousand fold bronze: I may not
count it; too long would be leisure for its numbering:
all that Kleitor gave, and Tegea, the towering cities of the
Achaians;
all that the Lykaian sanctuary by the field of Zeus set to be
won by strength of foot or of hand.

Since Kastor came to Pamphaës' entertainment
and Polydeukes his brother, it is no marvel
that to be good athletes runs in their blood. The lords
of Sparta and the wide dancing lawns dispose
the ordinances of games in their beauty, with Herakles and
with Hermes beside them.
They care for men that are righteous. Indeed, the race of the
gods fails not their friends.

They with life changing to and fro dwell one day beside
their father beloved,
Zeus, and the day that follows under the secret places of the
earth in the hollows of Therapne.
The destiny they fulfil is the same; such
was the choice of Polydeukes rather than be god indeed
and dwell in the sky, when Kastor fell in the fighting,
whom Idas, angered over some driving of cattle, stabbed
with the bronze spearhead.

Lynkeus, staring from Taÿgetos, saw them hiding
in an oak tree, for beyond all mortals else his eye
was sharpest. And in ravening speed of their feet
they came down and devised at once a monstrous act,
and terribly did these sons of Aphareus suffer at the hands
of Zeus; for straightway
Leda's son, Polydeukes, came pursuing, and they stood at
bay by their father's tomb.

Ripping aloft the dedication of death, the smoothed grave-
   stone,
they cast it at Polydeukes' chest, but availed not to shatter
nor drive him back. He, leaping with quick spear,
buried the bronze in Lynkeus' side,
and Zeus on Idas crashed the flame of the smoking thunder-
   bolt.
These two burned, forlorn. Men find strife bitter when they
   undertake those who are stronger.

With speed Tyndareus' son ran back to his mighty brother,
and found him not dead, drawing yet some shuddering
   breath of life.
In grief, letting fall hot tears,
he cried aloud: "Kronion, my father, what release
shall there be from sorrow? Grant death also to me with this
   man, my lord.
Bereft of his friends a man's honor is gone. Few mortals are
   steadfast in distress

"to endure hardship." He spoke, and Zeus came near
and answered: "You are my son; but thereafter her lord, a
   hero,
embracing your mother, shed seed that is mortal:
this man. Behold: of these two things I give you choice
entire; if you would escape death and age that all men hate,
to dwell beside me on Olympos with Athene and Ares of the
   black spear,

"that right is yours. But if all your endeavor is for
your twin, and you would have in all things shares alike,
half the time you may breathe under the earth,
half the time in the golden houses of the sky."
He spoke, and no twofold counsel divided the hero's heart,
but he set free from darkness the eyes of Kastor of the
   brazen belt, and his voice thereafter.

NEMEA 11

Daughter of Rhea, mistress appointed of prytanies, Hestia:
sister of Zeus on high and of Hera, his queen and consort,
with favor welcome into your house Aristagoras,
with favor also near your bright scepter his companions,
who honor you as they keep Tenedos upright,

propitiating you first of goddesses with much libation
and smoke of victims; the lyre murmurs deep among them,
   and singing;
the right of Zeus the Hospitable is wrought at their quenchless
feasting tables. But in honor let him pass
the twelve-month period with heart not torn.

I bless this man for Agesilas, his father,
for the splendor and linked serenity of his limbs.
Yet if one, keeping wealth, surpass in beauty likewise
and show his strength by excellence in the games,
let him yet remember the limbs he appoints are mortal
and that he must put upon him earth, the end of all things.

In the speech of good citizens he should win praise
and be a theme of elaboration in the deep, sweet singing.
From contests among the neighbors, sixteen times
shining successes have garlanded Aristagoras
and his city in fair repute for wrestling and the vaunting
   pankration.

The hopes too hesitant of his parents kept their son's strength
from endeavor in the games at Pytho and Olympia.
By oath, I say, to my thinking had he ventured
beside Kastalia and the grove of the slope of Kronos,
he had come back in glory beyond his straining antagonists;

he had kept the revel of the five-year cycle ordained
by Herakles, and bound his hair in the shining
branches. But one man, light-minded, vaunting hopes
drive from the good; another one, who blames overmuch
his own strength, the undaring spirit drags at his hand
to falter him back from splendors that are his by right.

It were easy to guess the blood from Sparta and from
Peisandros of old, who came from Amyklai with Orestes,
leading hither a host of Aiolians in their brazen gear,
and from the waters of Ismenos a mixed strain
by Melanippos on his mother's side. But the valors rooted of
    old,

interchanging, reveal the strength in the generations of men.
Neither in the soil do the black plow-acres
nor orchards in every circling year consent to yield
blossoming and fragrance equal in richness,
but in seasons alternate. The same destiny controls

mortality. From Zeus comes no clear sign
to men. Even so we go abroad in our manhood's height,
pondering many designs; for our limbs are shackled to shame-
    less
hope, and the streams of forethought lie afar.
We should seek out some measure in things gained;
too bitter are the pangs of madness after loves that are past
    attainment.

ISTHMIA 1

Thebes of the golden shield, my mother, I will put
your errand beyond other necessity that is upon me.
Let not Delos of the rocks that is my delight
begrudge me; for what delights the good
more than parents in their graciousness? Give way,
island of Apollo; by God's grace I shall achieve a twofold
   task, the delight of both,

making a song of dancing to Phoibos of the uncut hair
in wave-washed Keos among the men of the sea,
likewise for the Isthmos, that shoulder that dykes the surf.
It has granted garlands from games won
six times to the host of the sons of Kadmos, splendor
of fair success for their own land, on whose soil Alkmana
   bore a child

fearless, for the savage hounds of Geryon shivered before him.
But I will give Herodotos his meed for the four-horse chariot
   race;
and for reins guided by no hands other than his own
I will implicate him in song for Kastor or Iolaos.
These two in Lakedaimon and Thebes were the mightiest
   charioteers among heroes.

In all trials of strength they won most prizes,
and their houses were made magnificent with tripods,
cauldrons, dishes of gold. The feel
of garlands given in token of victory
was theirs. That excellence is a clear shining
they had alike in the naked race and the course of warriors
   among clattering shields,

for the way of the javelin's flight thrown from their hands
and the cast of the stone discus.
There was no pentathlon then, but for each event
the end lay in itself.
And often and again, binding their brows with the clustered
branched garlands, by Dirke's waters they appeared; and
  beside Eurotas,

the son of Iphikles, dweller among the breed of the Sown
  Men;
and among Achaians Kastor the Tyndarid of the high house
  at Therapne.
Farewell both: I must bring the sweep of my song about
to Poseidon and the holy Isthmos and the strands of On-
  chestos,
to speak aloud in this man's honor the glorious destiny of
  Asopodoros, his father,

and Orchomenos with its ancestral acres
that in sympathy accepted him, he
being stricken and in the unhappiness of shipwreck,
out of the sea immeasurable; now
the fortune in this house has come back, to stand
once more high in its happiness of old; the man who has
  had labor of mind wins forethought also.

But if every temper of him is disposed toward virtue
both ways, by outlay and endurance of toil,
toward such finding the goal we should bring lordly
praise, freely and with heart not begrudging;
for it is a light gift for a man well skilled
to find the right word for various labors achieved and build
  up splendor in all men's sight.

And, in truth, each man delights in the price befitting work
  done—

shepherd, plowman, fowler, or one who lives by the sea.
The strain of warding off incessant hunger is on all men,
but he who in contests or in war achieves the delicate glory
is magnified to be given the supreme prize, splendor of
    speech from citizen and stranger.

It befits us now to hymn the son of Kronos
the earth-shaker, our neighbor and benefactor,
in requital, the lord of the running of horses,
and to speak, Amphitryon,
of your sons, and the hollow of Minyas,
and the glorious grove of Demeter, Eleusis, and Euboia,
    where the ways curve;

your precinct in Phylake, Protesilaos, I bring likewise,
yours, and of the Achaian men.
But to speak of all that Hermes, god of games,
has bestowed on Herodotos
for horses racing, the song's measure is straitened
to prevent me. Indeed, many a time the thing left silent
    makes for happiness.

May he be lifted on the shining wings of the Muses,
the melodious, and fill his hands with choice leafage won
from Pytho also and Olympian games by Alpheos, and
    bring honor
upon seven-gated Thebes. But if a man keep wealth a secret
    thing in his house
and laugh at each encounter, he knows not that he appoints
    to Hades a life without glory.

132

ISTHMIA 2

Thrasyboulos, the men of old who mounted the chariot
of the golden-veiled Muses with the ringing lyre in their
  hands
lightly loosed the shafts of their delicate love-songs
for those who were beautiful in the delight and pride
upon them to waken enthroned Aphrodite.

The Muse in those days was not mercenary nor worked for
  hire,
nor was the sweetness of Terpsichore's honeyed singing for
  sale
nor her songs with faces silvered over for their soft utter-
  ance.
Nowadays she drives us to hold with that Argive's
word, that mounts close to the truth itself.

Money is man, he said, forlorn alike of possessions and
  friends.
But you are wise; you know whereof I sing—
an Isthmian victory with horses
Poseidon granted to Xenokrates,
sending a wreath of Dorian parsley
to bind on his hair in token of triumph;

grace to a great man of chariots and light of Akragas.
And, at Krisa, mighty Apollo looked down upon him and
  gave him splendor,
and he met the famed favor of the sons of Erechtheus
at shining Athens, with no cause to blame
the hand of the charioteer that steered well the car,

133

Nikomachos, handling in skill all reins.
Zeus Kronios' heralds of the season of sacred truce
acclaimed him, men of Elis, who had known his hospitality
    of old;
and with glad outcry they hailed him,
gathered to the knees of golden Victory

in their land men call the grove of Olympian Zeus.
There the children of Ainesidamos
were made intimate with immortal honors.
For your house, Thrasyboulos, is no stranger
to the loveliness of such festivals,
nor to the sweet affirmation in songs of praise.

Nowise rocky nor steep is the path we take
to bring home to men of reputation the glories of the Muses
    of Helikon.
I have spun the discus far and thus far also would cast the
    spear, to tell
how beyond all men gentle was the temper Xenokrates
used in his time; a modest man among citizens

whose horsemanship was in the style to be known among all
    Hellenes;
and all the festivals of the gods he embraced, nor did any
    gale's blast
strike his sail at the hospitality of his board.
For summer's venture he passed the Phasis,
and the Nile headlands for the winter sailing.

Now, though envious hopes flutter over the minds of mortals,
let Thrasyboulos not be silenced over his father's excellence;
nor silence yet these songs. I did not make them
that they might rest in sleep.
All these things, Nikasippos, dispense
when you come to Thrasyboulos, the friend of my heart.

ISTHMIA 3

If any man be fortunate in the glory of games
or strength of riches, and yet check down bitter excess in his
    heart,
it is his to be wrapped in the praise of his city's men.
Great prowess descends upon mortals,
Zeus, from you; the prosperity of the worshipful lives long;
    but those whose hearts are aslant,
with them it stays not long to wax and blossom.

In requital for great things done we must praise the noble in
    song,
and in our acclamation lift them high with the gentle Graces.
It is Melissos' destiny for twofold success
to turn his heart toward the sweetness of satisfaction.
In the glades of Isthmos he was given garlands, and in the
    fold of the valley
of the deep-breasted lion he made Thebes to be acclaimed

by conquering in the chariot race. He refutes not
the virtue in men's blood engendered.
Know that, of old, Kleonymos
was famed for chariots;
and they of his mother's side, akin to the children of Labda-
    kos,
advanced laboring their wealth on the four-horsed car.
But time, in the turning-over of days, works change for better
    or worse; the unwounded are God's children.

ISTHMIA 4

Multitudinous are the ways the gods have given,
O Melissos, to follow in song the achievements of you and
    yours,
such crafty strength did you show at the Isthmos,
in which, flowering forever, the race of Kleonymos,
with God favoring, have gone to the mortal end of life;
    except that the changing winds
burst forth variously to drive all men at will.

From the beginning they have been men of honor in Thebes,
friends of strangers in neighbor cities, free of vaunting
pride; in all testimonies borne on the winds among men
for unfailing reputation of those that are gone
and the living also, they have come to the uttermost goal; in
    the height of virtue
by pride of blood they touch the pillars of Herakles.

Further than this no man can drive his strength.
These were skilled in horsemanship;
they were pleasing in the sight of Ares the brazen.
But in the space of one day the bitter
snowstorm of battle made desolate
that blessed hearth of four men.
Now once more it is as when, after the winter darkness, the
    months change
and earth flowers again in the crimson of roses

by the gods' behest. And the shaker of the earth, who dwells
    in Onchestos
and the sea bridge beside the ramparts of Korinth,
granting this song of acclamation to their race,

rouses as from its bed their ancient glory
for splendid things achieved. It had fallen asleep; but, waken-
    ing now, it waxes to brilliance,
shining forth as the dawn star among others.

Beside the hills of Athens it had heralded the chariot victory,
and in the games of Adrastos at Sikyon it granted
such drifting leaves of song among men of that generation;
nor did they keep their curved chariot from the communal
    games
of all the Hellenes, but strove joyously with lavish expense
    on horses.
Silence of obscurity descends on those who will not endeavor,

but even among strivers there may be darkness of luck
before they come to the utmost goal.
The gifts of chance are various and they change.
Also the skill of small men
has thrown the stronger by stealth of sudden attack. Witness
the might of Aias that he himself slaughtered
by dead of night with the thrust of his own sword,
and has got reproach among the sons of the Hellenes who
    went to Troy.

Yet Homer has glorified him beyond other men,
and straightened the story of his valor in the rhapsode's
magic words to charm all men thereafter.
A thing said walks in immortality
if it has been said well; and over the fruitful earth and across
    the sea
fares the light that dies never of splendid deeds.

May the Muses give me gracious aid to light such a beacon
    of song
for Melissos also, a garland for the scion of Telesiadas
worthy his pankratiast's strength. For daring of heart,

in action, he is like thunderous lions among beasts,
but, for cunning, the fox that falls on his back to foil the
    eagle's plunge.
All means are fair to baffle the adversary.

He was not given Orion's stature;
rather he is a mean man by his look,
but hard to grapple in strength.
Once before, in the Libyan cornlands,
there came from Kadmeian Thebes to the house of Antaios
a man small in stature, inflexible of will,
to wrestle him and put an end to that building
with skulls of strangers the temple to Poseidon.

It was Herakles, Alkmana's son, who scaled Olympos, who
    knew
all earth, and sounded the deeply veiled abyss of the gray sea
to make easy the passage for sailors.
Now he dwells in bliss and magnificence beside
the lord of the aegis, honored and beloved among immortals,
    with Hebe to wife,
master in a house of gold and son-in-law to Hera.

To him beside the Elektran gate his citizens have dedicated
    a feast
and the freshly built circle of altars; there we feed
the fires for his eight bronze-armored sons who died,
sons that Megara bore him, Kreon's daughter.
In their honor the flames rise up at sunset to shine nightlong
and beat the air with billows of fragrant smoke.

And the second day is given to the issue of annual games
and the work that is for men's strength.
There the head of Melissos has been made bright
with myrtle garlands twice for victory,
once before for success among boys his age.
He heeded the deep counsel of his trainer,
who guided him; to both, Melissos and Orseas now,
I will make my song of triumph and drench them in grace
    and delight.

ISTHMIA 5

Mother of Helios, Theia the many-named:
for your sake men have made the great strength of gold
to be a thing prized above other possessions.
And ships that strive on the sea
and horses under the chariot, by your grace, lady,
are made wonderful in the rapid whirl of contests.

She among the assembled games has made
glory to be a lovely thing, when the clustering garlands
are bound over a man's head, for success in strength
of hand, or speed of his feet.
The crucial strength is given of the gods to men;
but two things only there are that minister to the brightest
   bloom of life as wealth blossoms:

success and the good speech that a man hears of himself.
Strive not to become Zeus; you have everything
if destiny of such splendors befall you.
Mortals must be content with mortality.
For you, Phylakidas, a twofold blossoming of power
at the Isthmos is laid away in time, and at Nemea for you
and Pytheas, your brother, pankratiasts. My heart
has no traffic here in songs not of the Aiakidai;
but with the Graces to guide me I have come to the sons of
   Lampon,

to this just island. If she is turned to a pure way
in actions whose springs are of God,
spare not to mingle the glorification becoming
to song for struggles achieved.
For even among the heroes those fighters who were brave

have gained by praise; they are made famous by lyres, in the
   many-voiced symphony of flutes

into time without end; in their worshipfulness they have
   given
to singers, by God's grace, the themes of their art.
At the shining sacrifices of the Aitolians
the great children of Oineus,
at Thebes Iolaos the charioteer,
have honor; Perseus at Argos; Kastor's spear and Polydeukes
   beside the waters of Eurotas.

Here at Aigina it is the great hearts
of Aiakos and his sons. Embattled
twice, they sacked the city of the Trojans, following
Herakles that first time,
thereafter with the Atreidai. Take flight now from earth.
Say, who slew Kyknos, Hektor,
the fearless marshal of Aithiopian men,
Memnon armored in bronze? Who wounded
brave Telephos with the spear, at the Kaïkos banks?

Therefore, my lips give them to their land, Aigina,
the glorious island, a tower builded from time
primeval, for the highest valors to storm.
There are many arrows of song
my speech has skill to sound forth in their honor.
Today the city of Aias, defended in battle by sailors, will
   speak for them,

Salamis, in God's rain and the bloody death-sleet,
where numberless men went down.
Nevertheless, drench arrogance in silence.
Not all the things Zeus gives are of one kind,
and Zeus is master of all. But as the loveliness
of honey are the honors that greet such glad victories. Let a
   man

strive in games, learning of the seed
of Kleonikos. The long labors of these men
are not blinded in time, nor did reckoning
of expense make cautious their hopes.
I praise Pytheas also among fighters for showing
his brother the battering strokes' pattern—
a man skilful with his hands, and of mind also.
Take for him the garland and the fleecy headband,
and with him bring home the young song with its wings.

ISTHMIA 6

As in the splendor of a revel of men,
we mix a second bowl of the strains of the Muses
for the sake of Lampon's race and all its triumphs. Zeus, in
    your own Nemea first
we held up before you the shining of their garlands;
and now again before the lord of the Isthmos
and the fifty Nereids, for the youngest boy,
Phylakidas, has won. May the third time be
such that we make at Aigina our last libation
to Zeus Savior, Olympian, in the honeyed singing.

If any man, gladly lavishing gold
and toil, win to achievement of excellence given of God,
his destiny increases the loveliness of fame. At the uttermost
    fortunate strands
he drops anchor, moving in the eyes of God.
In mood like this, Lampon, son
of Kleonikos, makes his prayer to face and take death
and gray age; and I beseech Klotho that is throned on high
and her sister Fates to attend the supplication heard from
    afar
of this man, my beloved friend.

Sons of Aiakos, riders in chariots of gold,
I see as I set foot on this island the task
most clear before me, to shower you in praise.
Thousand fold are cut in the land the hundred-foot-wide
    roads of your great achievements,
even beyond the waters that feed the Nile,
among the Hyperboreans.
There is no city so barbarian or backward of speech

it knows nothing of the heroic fame of Peleus, the blessed
    son-in-law of the gods,

no city that knows not of Telamonian Aias
and his father. Alkmana's son, on his way by ship
to battle loud in bronze at Troy, a trial of fighters, took as a
    fain helper
Telamon with the men of Tiryns, to bring
vengeance upon Laomedon for his deceptions.
He took the city of Pergamon, and in the same hero's com-
    pany smote
the hosts of the Meropes and the oxherd mountain-high,
Alkyoneus, encountered in the Phlegraian Fields. The hand
of Herakles spared not the deep-voiced

bowstring. First summoning Aiakides
to the venture, he came on the young men at their feasting.
Strong Telamon saw him standing in the lion's skin, called
    in invitation
Amphitryoniadas of the heavy spear
to begin the outpouring of nectar, and put in his hands
a wine goblet cut in shuddering gold.
Herakles, lifting into the sky his invincible arms,
spoke aloud: "If ever before, Zeus my father,
you have been moved to listen kindly to prayer of mine,

"now, in divine supplication,
I entreat you, give this man by Eriboia a brave son
to be my guest and friend, and a destined man.
Grant him strength unbreakable like this beast hide that is
    wrapped about me,
this skin of a lion that, first of all my labors,
I killed at Nemea long ago.
Let his heart be such also." As he spoke the god sent
the lord of birds, a great eagle; and sweet delight troubled
    his heart within,

and he spoke aloud, as if he had been a seer:
"You shall have the child you ask for, my Telamon.
For the bird that showed him forth, call him mighty Aias, to
 be
in the tumult of armies a man of terror."
He spoke, and sat at their table.
It would be long for me to rehearse all the tale of their great
 deeds.
I have come, O Muse, to minister to Phylakidas
and Pytheas and Euthymenes their festal choruses. The Ar-
 give way
must be my way; the fewest words.

They have taken victories in the pankration
thrice at the Isthmos, at leafy Nemea,
these glorious young men with their uncle; such occasion,
 deserved of song, they have brought up into the light.
The land of the sons of Psalychos they water
with the shining rain of the Graces.
Steadying the house of Themistios, they dwell here in a city
that God loves. Lampon keeps the precept
of Hesiod, careful training toward achievement,
and tenders the saying urgently to his sons,

bringing therewith brilliance upon all his city.
Among strangers he is admired for his kindnesses.
His mind in pursuit and possession is temperate.
His speech keeps within purpose. You could say that as man
 among athletes he stood
as Naxian stone among others,
a hone to edge bronze.
I will give them to drink limpid water of Dirke, that the
 deep-girdled daughters
of Memory the golden-robed draw from the well beside
 the strong-flanked gates of Kadmos.

144

ISTHMIA 7

In which of your native splendors aforetime, Thebe,
blessed city, does your heart take most delight?
Was it when you raised up Dionysos
of the wide-floating hair, to be seated beside bronze-clashing
Demeter? Or when, by midnight, you welcomed the might-
    iest
of gods in the gold snowfall

that time he stood in the forecourts
of Amphitryon and approached his wife with the seed of
    Herakles in his body?
Or for the shrewd judgments of Teiresias?
Or for Iolaos and his horsemanship?
Or for the Sown Men of the spears that failed not? Or
    when, from the loud, strong battle,
you sent Adrastos home, forlorn

of his companions in their thousands to Argos, city of
    horses?
Or when you set on upright foot
the Dorian inroad,
Lakedaimonians, and the Aigeidai,
men sprung of your seed, took Amyklai by the prophecies
    of Pytho?
But grace that is grown old
sleeps, and men are forgetful

of that which issues not binding the high perfection
of poetry to bright streams of words.
Hail, then, in song sweetly chanted

Strepsiades also; for he brings home a victory
in the pankration won at Isthmos; a man tremendous in his
    strength and shapely to behold; and he carries courage
that shames not his stature.

The light of the violet-wreathing Muses is about him,
and he has offered his garland to be shared with his uncle
    and namesake,
whom Ares of the bronze shield gave his death,
though honor among good men is laid up against it.
Let him be sure, he who in that storm-cloud endures the
    bloody rain, for the sake
of his own beloved city,

and carries death into the hosts opposed,
magnifies the glory of his kindred citizens
living, and in death also.
You, son of Diodotos, chose the way
of Meleagros, a fighter; the way of Hektor
and Amphiaraos,
to breathe out your flowering youth

among the struggling champions, where the bravest
took the stern verdict of battle among the forlorn hopes
and endured sorrow I cannot speak of. But now
Poseidon, who folds the earth, has granted me calm
out of storm. I will sing this man as I lay the wreaths on his
    hair. Let no envy
of immortals break the bloom.

In quest of the fleeting delight
I walk softly into old age and the period
of doom. We die, all of us, alike;
but our destiny is not the same. If one look afar,
short is the way seen to reach the bronze-paved citadel of the
    gods. Yet Pegasos,
the winged, cast down

Bellerophon, his lord, when he strove to reach
the houses of the sky and the fellowship
of Zeus. An end in all bitterness awaits
the sweetness that is wrong.
But to us, Loxias, splendid in your golden hair, grant
in your own contests
the blossoming garland even at Pytho.

To Kleandros in the pride of his youth and in glorious
quittance, O young men, for his striving,
go now beside the shining porch of Telesarchos, his father,
    and wake
the song to give him gladness for Isthmian victory
and his strength proved at Nemean contests; and thereto I
    also, grieved though I be at heart, ask leave to call
the golden Muse. Slipped free of great sorrows,
let us not fall into desolation of garlands;
cherish not your grief; we have ceased from evils above our
    strength.
Let us communicate some sweetness even after the hardship,
since from above our heads
some god has turned aside that stone of Tantalos,

a weight Hellas could never dare. But now
the terror has gone by and taken
away the strong brooding in my heart; it is better always to
    watch what is close at hand
in everything. A treacherous age hangs over men's heads;
it makes crooked the way of life. But even this can be healed
    in man, with freedom. We must be of good hope.
A child of Thebes, the seven-gated,
should shed the glory of the Graces upon Aigina;
for these were twin daughters of one father, Asopos,
the youngest, and they pleased King Zeus;
and one he made to live by the lovely waters
of Dirke, queen over a city of chariots,

but you, Aigina, he carried away to Oinopia, the island,
and lay with you, and you bore to the lord
of the loud thunder the best of men on earth, brilliant Aiakos.
    He was judge

among the divinities even, and his godlike sons
and his sons' sons were warlike, pre-eminent to wield the
  bitter, clashing bronze in battle.
And they were temperate men with discretion in their hearts,
a thing remembered in the assemblies of the blessed ones
when Zeus and bright Poseidon came to strife over Thetis,
each desirous to be wed to her beauty
and possess her; the passion was on them.
But the will of the gods did not accomplish such union,

for they had heard things foretold. Themis,
lady of good counsel, rose up among them and spoke
how it was destined for this sea-goddess to bring to birth a
  lord
stronger than his father, to wield in his hand a shaft heavier
  than the thunderbolt
or the weariless trident, if she lay with Zeus or his brothers.
  "Let her go.
She must come rather into a mortal bed.
Let her look upon her son slain in battle,
but a son like Ares for strength of hand, like the thundershaft
  for speed of his feet.
For my part, I say grant the divine grace
of this marriage to Aiakos' son, Peleus,
rumored the most upright man that dwells in Iolkos plain.

"And let the messages go straightway
to Chiron's immortal cave.
Let not Nereus' daughter put twice in our hands the leaf-
  ballots of our contention.
By full moon at evening let her break
the fastening of her lovely virginity for the hero." The god-
  dess spoke before the Kronians; they
nodded with immortal brows. The words' harvest
faded not. They say the two kings consented
to Thetis' marriage; and the lips of poets

have published to those who knew not of it the young
    strength of Achilles;
who stained the Mysian vineyards
with the dark blood of Telephos, drenching the plain;

and made a bridge to bring the Atreidai home,
and set Helen free, cutting
with the spear's edge the sinews of Troy, that had fought
    him off in deadly battle
as he did great deeds in the plain; Memnon the mighty
and impetuous Hektor, others, chiefs among men; Achilles,
    the staunch Aiakid, showed them Persephone's house
and revealed the glory of Aigina and the stock he came of.
Even in death, songs did not leave him,
but, standing beside his pyre and his grave, the maidens
of Helikon let fall upon him their abundant dirge.
Even the immortals were pleased
to bestow on a brave man, though perished, the song of
    goddesses.

Such is the truth even now, while the chariot
of the Muses goes with speed to glorify
Nikokles in memory of his boxing. Honor him, who in the
    Isthmian glade
won the parsley wreath of the Dorians. He conquered the
    dwellers-about
with the stroke of that fist none could avoid. The choice
    blood of his cousin
does not shame him. Let one of his own age bind
on Kleandros' brow the delicate wreath
of myrtle for the pankration, for with success the games of
    Alkathöos ere now
and the youth at Epidauros accepted him.
A good man can give him all praise.
He has not thrust down his youth untried into a place where
    splendors are hidden.

NOTES ON THE ODES

OLYMPIA 1

For Hieron of Syracuse. Race for horse and rider (the famous race horse, Pherenikos, is named). 476 B.C. Pindar was probably in Sicily for the presentation of the work.

This is the first of the odes for Hieron and follows most nearly the normal pattern.

OLYMPIA 2

For Theron of Akragas in Sicily. Chariot race. 476 B.C. The same victory is also commemorated in *Olympia* 3.

There is no central myth; the various mythical allusions repeat incessantly the theme of some success won after great hardship and culminate in the description of the blessed life after death. Theron had been cruel as well as kind, unhappy as well as fortunate. In seeing allusions to this we are not likely to be wrong. The regular victory ode for this occasion is *Olympia* 3; this poem is a manner of consolation.

The allusion to the crows probably refers to Simonides and his nephew Bacchylides, though this has been disputed.

OLYMPIA 3

For the same person and victory as *Olympia* 2. 476 B.C.

Herakles, the hero of the myth, was the legendary founder of the Olympian games.

OLYMPIA 4

For Psaumis of Kamarina, in Sicily. Mule chariot race. Date uncertain.

OLYMPIA 5

For the same person and victory as *Olympia* 4. Date uncertain.

This is the only ode in the collection the authenticity of which has been questioned.

OLYMPIA 6

For Agesias of Syracuse. Mule chariot race. Probably 468 B.C.

Agesias, originally of Stymphalos in Arkadia, was a henchman of Hieron. He belonged to the family of the Iamidai, whose hereditary office as soothsayers is recorded down into Roman times. The myth tells the story of Iamos, the heroic ancestor who gave his name to the clan. The material, what with the double divine paternity and the twofold or threefold allegiance of Agesias, is exceptionally complicated; but the difficulties are met with triumphant, challenging, and almost perverse brilliance.

OLYMPIA 7

For Diagoras of Rhodes. Boxing. 464 B.C.
Diagoras is known to have been one of the exceptional athletes of his day. The rehearsal of his successes given here might be wearisome but is skilfully managed. The triple myth proceeds in a curious backward manner, the first episode recounted being the latest in time. All these parts embody the theme of success won, or granted by the gods, in spite of mistakes made. The appositeness of this may lie somewhere in the history of Diagoras or his family; if so, it is lost now.

OLYMPIA 8

For Alkimedon of Aigina. Boys' wrestling. 460 B.C.
The ode has the characteristic features of those written for Aiginetan victories: the emphasis on the justice and hospitality of the Dorian Aiginetans and the legendary presence of Aiakos or his descendants, who were friends of Herakles and the gods.
As in certain other poems for boy victors, the trainer appears—in this case Melesias, who has been shown to be an Athenian. At this time Athens and Aigina, who had fought indecisively a generation before, were on the brink of a war which was to cost the Aiginetans their freedom and, ultimately, their political existence. There can be no doubt where Pindar's sympathies lay; there is a sense of caution and strain in his praise of Melesias, who was his friend and who had other friends in Aigina (see *Nem.* 4 and 6).

OLYMPIA 9

For Epharmostos of Opous (Opountian Lokris). Wrestling. 468 B.C. The date is that of the Olympian victory itself; the actual presentation of the ode seems to have been delayed.
The main myth, difficult and not altogether clear, tells how Pyrrha and Deukalion repopulated the earth with stones, and of the begetting of the hero Opous by Zeus—apparently, two different myths concerning the origin of the Opountians, never successfully fused. The Homeric hero representing Lokris was Aias Oileus (not the great Aias), at whose festival the ode was produced. He might seem

152

to be the natural choice for myth-hero here, but Pindar barely mentions him in the last line, and that only because the occasion demanded it. Aias was famous, but his fame was not good.

The remarks on natural genius and acquired skill should be compared with those in the earlier *Olympia* 2. Here Pindar's views are greatly modified. The earlier passage was probably directed against Simonides, of whom there are several echoes in this poem. Echo often conveys compliment; is this a retraction and a peace offering?

OLYMPIA 10

For Agesidamos of Epizephyrian Lokris (in southern Italy). Boys' boxing. 476 B.C. This is the date of the victory; the execution of the ode was obviously long delayed. Pindar was probably in Sicily at the time and was very busy.

The myth tells of the first Olympic games, as founded by Herakles. There is less allusiveness and more simple chronicling than, perhaps, in any other Pindaric myth.

OLYMPIA 11

For the same person and victory as *Olympia* 10. 476 B.C. Either a brief preliminary offering to mitigate the foreseen postponement of the main ode or an additional piece thrown in by way of apology.

OLYMPIA 12

For Ergoteles of Himera. Distance run. 472 B.C.

Ergoteles, who had made his home in Sicilian Himera, was a political exile from Krete and thus a victim (in the end a happy one) of Fortune, whose concept dominates the poem.

OLYMPIA 13

For Xenophon of Korinth. Dash and pentathlon. 464 B.C.

The Korinthians appear as a nation of great inventors, and the myth appropriately tells how Bellerophon, a Korinthian hero, by divine aid discovered the bridle and rode the winged horse. The ode has its splendors; but there is so much to say about Korinth, and Xenophon and his family have won so many victories, that Pindar is somewhat overwhelmed.

OLYMPIA 14

For Asopichos of Orchomenos. Dash. 476 B.C. is the date given, but it has been questioned.

Such development of the invocation in so short a poem is unparalleled. This is one of Pindar's most splendid avowals of his belief that all human excellence comes by divine dispensation. What the Graces mean to him is so vivid that they almost come alive in his hands.

PYTHIA 1

For Hieron of Syracuse. Chariot race. 470 B.C.

Two years earlier, Hieron had founded a new city near and named after Mount Aitna and had established his son, Deinomenes, as king. Pindar is far more preoccupied with this foundation than with the victory.

There is no central myth, but mythical pictures and examples are scattered throughout the poem. The close is probably addressed to young Deinomenes rather than to Hieron.

PYTHIA 2

For Hieron of Syracuse. Chariot race. Date uncertain. This ode has been included in the Pythian corpus, but it is for no Pythian victory; perhaps for one in games at Syracuse. The poem is probably later than *Olympia* 1, certainly earlier than *Pythia* 1 and 3. There seems to be an allusion to Hieron driving his chariot in person, which places it before the deadly sickness we hear of in the First and Third Pythians.

The vivid myth of Ixion is, like other myths in the odes for Hieron, somewhat sinister; but the compliments which follow seem sincere and open. The bearing of the quasi-dialogue at the close remains a puzzle, though the meaning is clear enough.

PYTHIA 3

For Hieron of Syracuse. Apparently neither Pythian nor victory ode. A win at Pytho is mentioned but sounds remote. Date uncertain; but the illness spoken of in *Pythia* 1 (470 B.C.) has become hopeless. 468 B.C. is a possible date.

In the myth of Asklepios and his mother we may hear the same note of warning against vanity and restlessness that sounds in the stories of Tantalos and Ixion; in the rest, sympathy and regret. The ode reads like a letter of farewell.

PYTHIA 4

For Arkesilas of Kyrene. Chariot race. 462 B.C. The same occasion is commemorated in *Pythia* 5.

The circumstances that produced this ode are special. Damophilos of Kyrene, a kinsman of the young king Arkesilas, had been banished as the result of a quarrel. On the occasion of the king's victory he commissioned Pindar, his friend, to write this extraordinary ode, which closes with an eloquent plea for the restoration of Damophilos. Despite the compliments at the close, there is an unmistakable undercurrent of warning, which justifies the connecting of Damophilos' banishment with political upheavals, which, a few years later, cost Arkesilas his life.

The tale of Jason and the winning of the Fleece is linked to Arkesilas through the presence aboard the Argo of Euphamos, ancestor of the Kyrenaian dynasty. Despite the unprecedented length of the myth, the full story is not told, even in summary; we find, rather, a series of brilliant episodes, of which the first in the poem, and the latest in time, dramatizes the claim of the Battiad kings to Kyrene through the person of Euphamos.

PYTHIA 5

For the same person and victory as *Pythia* 4. 462 B.C.

This is the regular victory ode, commissioned by Arkesilas himself. The charioteer, his kinsman Karrhotos, is unusually prominent, being a man of mark (Arkesilas, though an expert, was no more able than Hieron of Syracuse to leave his domain and compete in person). The myth deals with Battos, colonizer and first king of Kyrene.

PYTHIA 6

For Xenokrates of Akragas. Chariot race. 490 B.C.

Xenokrates was brother and colleague of Theron, ruler of Akragas (Second and Third Olympians). Thrasyboulos, his son and Pindar's close friend (see *Isth*. 2) was the charioteer.

PYTHIA 7

For Megakles of Athens. Chariot race. 486 B.C.

Megakles was a member of the Alkmaionidai, a family of great political distinction at Athens. It is surprising that a Pythian chariot victory by this rich and famous man occasioned so short an ode.

PYTHIA 8

For Aristomenes of Aigina. Wrestling. Traditional and probable date, 446 B.C., making it, in all likelihood, the last of the victory odes.

If the traditional date is right, Aigina was at this time a member of the Athenian alliance, under Athenian domination. Right-wing Aiginetans like Aristomenes may well have had other ideas, and the crash of the giant Porphyrion may represent a necessarily veiled and wishful allusion to the possible downfall of Athens.

This is the only Aiginetan ode in which the Aiakidai do not hold the central position, although they are invoked at the close. The appearance of Alkmaion to Pindar (in a dream or vision?) seems to have dictated his place in the ode.

PYTHIA 9

For Telesikrates of Kyrene. Armored race. 478 B.C.

The initial myth speaks for itself and dominates the poem. The terminal myth also deals with marriage, and it is hard to resist the conclusion that romance was in the air for Telesikrates.

PYTHIA 10

For Hippokleas of Thessaly. Boys' two-lap race. Hippokleas is said to have won the single-lap dash also, but it is not mentioned in this poem. 498 B.C.

This is probably Pindar's earliest victory ode, written when he was only twenty. Neither the young victor nor his victories were of enormous importance, but it was a chance for the poet. Pindar also addresses himself to the boy's patron, Thorax, a great Thessalian nobleman, who was later to be guilty of inviting the Persian invasion.

At twenty, Pindar had already articulated beliefs which he was to hold through life: in blood and family, in the power of the gods, in the perilous position of human life and happiness.

PYTHIA 11

For Thrasydaios of Thebes. Boys' dash. Date variously given as 474 and 454 B.C. The question has not been settled.

The myth of Klytaimnestra and Orestes is, of course, that dealt with by Aeschylus in the Oresteia triology (456 B.C.). There are minor differences in Pindar's account, which, if the later date be accepted, may be meant as corrections of the version by Aeschylus. Pindar's is vivid enough, but why he should use the story at all in this ode is a mystery. It has nothing to do with Thebes, whose rich traditions Pindar knew by heart; it is entered through an unusually weak transition; and Pindar himself at the close seems to wonder why he brought it in. It may for some reason have been stipulated in the contract, which would account for the remarks on writing for hire.

Near the end of the poem, Pindar seems to feel that he must defend himself against charges of bad patriotism and unsound policy. The reference may be to his friendship with Hieron or Arkesilas, once more in the capacity of hired poet.

156

PYTHIA 12

For Midas of Akragas. Flute contest. 486 B.C.

NEMEA 1

For Chromios of Aitna. Chariot race. Date uncertain; but, since Chromios is called a citizen of Aitna, it must be later than the foundation of that city in 472 B.C.

Chromios was one of Hieron's captains, and his fighting abilities and hard work brought him wealth and honor. Here, at the close of the myth of Herakles and in *Nemea* 9 for the same Chromios, is the theme of rest and enjoyment after work well done.

NEMEA 2

For Timodamos of Acharnai (near Athens). Pankration. Date not given.

NEMEA 3

For Aristokleides of Aigina. Pankration. Date not given; but the language in places recalls that of *Olympia* 2 (476 B.C.).

NEMEA 4

For Timasarchos of Aigina. Boys' wrestling. Date not given but probably earlier than *Olympia* 8 (460 B.C.).

The story of Peleus and Hippolyta is told more explicitly in *Nemea* 5.

NEMEA 5

For Pytheas of Aigina. Pankration. Date not given, but probably shortly before the Battle of Salamis (480 B.C.). The subsequent victories of Pytheas' younger brother are commemorated in *Isthmian* 5 and 6.

The myth is interesting in that it explains why the Aiakidai— Peleus and Telamon—left Aigina. They had killed their half-brother, Phokos. The righteousness of Peleus is, however, vindicated in the story of his repulse of Hippolyta.

NEMEA 6

For Alkimidas of Aigina. Boys wrestling. Date not given.

NEMEA 7

For Sogenes of Aigina. Boys' pentathlon. Date not given.

Two mythical passages are of interest. In the first, Pindar, as elsewhere (*Nem.* 8, *Isth.* 4), defends Aias against Odysseus, as the strong and forthright man against the clever congenital liar. In the second he corrects himself for having (in the Sixth Paian) spoken too harshly of Neoptolemos, Achilleus' son. Neoptolemos was a cruel warrior, who cut down the aged Priam without mercy; but he was son to Achilleus, therefore one of the Aiakidai and a hero dear to the hearts of Pindar's Aiginetan friends. Pindar will not admit that he has made any mistake, but his concern is so great that it haunts the latter part of the poem and bursts out again at the close. This is an effective illustration of the seriousness with which the Greeks took their heroic legends.

NEMEA 8

For Deinias of Aigina. Two-lap race. Date not given.

The myth of Aias, who is defended against Odysseus, turns into a diatribe against invidious citizens or, perhaps, Pindar's personal enemies.

NEMEA 9

For Chromios of Aitna. Chariot race, at Sikyon, not Nemea. Date not given, but shortly after 472 B.C., as the foundation of Aitna in that year is called "recent." Chromios is the winner of a chariot race, celebrated in the First Nemean.

Amphiaraos, the one just man among the Seven against Thebes, is a favorite of Pindar's, though an "enemy."

NEMEA 10

For Theaios of Argos. Wrestling, at the Argive Hekatomboia, not Nemea. Date not given, but the poem is usually considered to be late.

This is the first and only ode for a winner from Argos, a city so rich in legendary traditions that the invocation rings throughout with heroic names. It is curious that the myth ultimately chosen is that of Kastor and Polydeukes, who were strictly Lakedaimonians and Argives only in the wider sense.

NEMEA 11

For Aristagoras of Tenedos. Not Nemean or a victory ode (although Aristagoras is an athlete whose achievements are praised). The occasion is the installation of the annual "prytanis" at Tenedos.

The poem follows, in general, the outline of the epinician ode but is almost wholly personal. There is no myth.

ISTHMIA 1

For Herodotos of Thebes. Chariot race. Date not given; but the allusions to misfortunes and exile may well refer to political upheavals at Thebes in and after 480 B.C.

Herodotos had driven the chariot himself, so that the praise of Iolaos and Kastor, great athletes of the heroic age, is apposite. Pindar postponed the writing of a poem for the Delians (possibly the Twelfth Paian) in order to finish this ode; there are few Theban victories in his list, and they meant much to him.

ISTHMIA 2

For Xenokrates of Akragas. Chariot race. Date not given, but approximately 470 B.C.

Xenokrates and his son Thrasyboulos are the victors of *Pythia* 6 (490 B.C.). Xenokrates had apparently died in the interval between this victory and the completion of this poem, which was sent overseas through Nikasippos and was addressed to Thrasyboulos, Pindar's friend. The personal bond between the two men probably accounts for the interesting tone of apology in the opening. Pindar hates to charge his friend a stiff price, or any price at all, but he must live.

ISTHMIA 3

For Melissos of Thebes. Chariot race at Nemea. See *Isthmia* 4, with which this poem forms a single piece.

ISTHMIA 4

For Melissos of Thebes. Pankration. Date uncertain but thought to be later than 479 B.C., since the death of members of the house in battle and attendant misfortunes are best referred to the Battle of Plataia and the period thereafter.

Melissos, it appears, won a victory in the pankration at the Isthmos and commissioned Pindar to write the ode. Before it had been presented, Melissos won the chariot race at Nemea, which occasioned the addition of a triad at the beginning of the poem. This triad is *Isthmia* 3. The two parts are identical in metrical structure.

After so many handsome and stately athletes, it comes as a shock to hear Melissos described as not much to look at. He appears to have been a small, tough, and probably dirty fighter; and Pindar must have known him well to speak so frankly, though the passage is complimentary in a left-handed way. It is no less a shock to hear that Herakles was small, but there was an independent tradition to that effect.

159

ISTHMIA 5

For Phylakidas of Aigina. Pankration. Date, shortly after the battle of Salamis (480 B.C.), in which Herodotos records that the Aiginetan contingent was awarded the prize for valor.

Nemea 5 celebrates the victory of Pytheas, Phylakidas' elder brother, and *Isthmia* 6 a previous win by Phylakidas. This is the last of the series.

ISTHMIA 6

For Phylakidas of Aigina. Boys' pankration. Date, shortly before the Battle of Salamis, perhaps in the same year (480 B.C.). For the circumstances see *Isthmia* 5.

The myth of Telamon proceeds backward to the point at which Herakles prays for and predicts the birth of a great son, Aias, to his friend.

ISTHMIA 7

For Strepsiades of Thebes. Pankration. Date not given; but the battle of which Pindar speaks in the poem has been thought, with good reason, to be the one fought in 457 B.C. at Oinophyta, in which Athens defeated the Thebans and won control of Boiotia. Pindar's allusion to his own advanced age supports this.

For myth is substituted the heroic death in this battle of Strepsiades' uncle of the same name, with the recollection of Meleager, Hektor, and Amphiaraos, all brave men who lost. On this interpretation, the fall of Bellerophon is—like the fall of Porphyrion in *Pythia* 8—an allusion aimed at Athens.

ISTHMIA 8

For Kleandros of Aigina. Boys' pankration. Date not given, but almost certainly 478 B.C. The Theban Pindar's mixed feelings of relief and sorrow over the outcome of the Persian War are nowhere made more plain.

The myth constitutes a particularly clear and explicit chapter in the life of Pindar's beloved Aiakid hero, Peleus.

GLOSSARY OF NAMES

This glossary is not an exhaustive index. It is intended simply as a guide to the better understanding of Pindar's references. Accents on names are not quantitative but denote syllabic stress as used in making this translation.

ABAS. Legendary king of Argos. *Pyth.* 8.

ADRAS'TOS. King of Argos, who led the Seven against Thebes. *See* POLYNEIKES. *Ol.* 6, *Pyth.* 8, etc.

AGE'SIAS. Victor, *Ol.* 6.

AGESI'DAMOS. Victor. *Ol.* 10, 11.

AGESI'DAMOS. Father of Chromios. *Nem.* 1, 9.

AGLAI'A. One of the Graces. *Ol.* 14.

AI'AKOS. Son of Zeus and Aigina, father of Peleus and Telamon (also of Phokos), who, with their descendants, are called the "Aiakidai." *Ol.* 8, *Pyth.* 8, etc.

AIGAI. A place in Achaia, sacred to Poseidon. *Nem.* 5.

AI'GEIDAI. "The sons of Aigeus," a clan in Thebes to which Pindar belonged (*Pyth.* 5). They assisted in the Dorian conquest of Lakedaimon and in the colonization of Thera and, thence, of Kyrene. Thus there were branches of the Aigeidai in all those places. *Pyth.* 5, *Isth.* 7.

AIGI'MIOS. Ancestor of the Dorians, who befriended Hyllos, the son of Herakles. *Pyth.* 1, 5.

AIGIS'THOS. Klytaimnestra's lover, killed by Orestes. *Pyth.* 11.

AINE'AS. Presumably a Stymphalian, the leader of the chorus which performed *Olympia* 6.

AINESI'DAMOS. Father of Theron. *Ol.* 2, 3; *Isth.* 2.

AIO'LIANS. A Greek tribe said to have migrated from Boiotia and Thessaly to Asia Minor and the islands near by. *Ol.* 1, *Nem.* 11, etc.

AI'OLOS. Ancestor of Jason. *Pyth.* 4.

AITNA. Mount Etna; also, a city of the same name near the mountain, founded by Hieron as the domain of his son, Deinomenes. *Pyth.* 1, etc.

AITO'LIAN. Aitolia was a district of northwestern Greece. The inhabitants of Elis claimed Aitolian descent. *Ol.* 3, *Isth.* 5.

AKAS'TOS. King of the Minyai and lord of Iolkos, who attempted to murder Peleus. *Nem.* 4, 5.

ALA'TAS. A primeval king of Korinth. *Ol.* 13.

ALEU'AS. Father or ancestor of Thorax. The family were known as the Aleuadai. *Pyth.* 10.

ALEXI'BIOS. Father of Karrhotos. *Pyth.* 5.

ALKAI'OS. Father of Amphitryon, grandfather (putative) of Herakles. *Ol.* 6.

ALKI'MEDON. Victor, *Ol.* 8.

ALKI'MIDAS. Victor, *Nem.* 6.

161

ALKMA'NA. Mother of Herakles. *Ol.* 7, *Nem.* 1, etc.

ALKMA'ON. Son of Amphiaraos. *Pyth.* 8.

ALKYO'NEUS. A giant, struck down by Herakles. *Nem.* 4, *Isth.* 6.

AL'PHEOS. The river which flows by Olympia. *Ol.* 1, 2, 3, etc.

A'MENAS. A stream on which the city of Aitna was built. *Pyth.* 1.

AMMON. An Egyptian god identified with Zeus. *Pyth.* 4.

AMPHIARA'OS. One of the Seven against Thebes (*see* POLYNEIKES). A sooth-sayer who foresaw the disastrous end of the expedition, he went against his will and was considered the one virtuous man in a violent and godless company. As he fled in the rout, the earth opened before his chariot and engulfed him alive, after which he was worshiped as a divine, oracular hero. *Ol.* 6, *Pyth.* 8, *Nem.* 9, *Isth.* 7.

AMPHITRI'TE. A sea-goddess, wife of Poseidon. *Ol.* 6.

AMPHITRYO'NIADAS. Herakles, putative son of Amphitryon. *Isth.* 6.

AMY'KLAI. A fortress near Sparta, once independent; in Pindar (not in Homer or Attic tragedy) the home of Agamemnon. *Pyth.* 1, 11; *Isth.* 7.

ANTAI'OS. King of Irasa. *Pyth.* 9.

ANTAI'OS. A giant who wrestled with Herakles and was killed by him. *Isth.* 4.

ANTI'LOCHOS. Son of Nestor, killed at Troy by Memnon while rescuing his father. *Pyth.* 6.

APHA'REUS. Father of Idas and Lynkeus. *Nem.* 10.

ARCHI'LOCHOS. Of Paros, a poet who lived probably in the early seventh century B.C. (date uncertain and much disputed). Enough of his work remains to indicate that he was a first-rate poet, powerful and original; but it is clear that Pindar disapproved of him. He was illegitimate, followed the calling of a professional soldier, and was probably well acquainted with poverty and unhappiness. He was particularly famous for talents in satire and invective, as Pindar also indicates. His fragments show such talent, but much besides. *Ol.* 9, *Pyth.* 2

ARETHOU'SA. A spring on Ortygia. *Pyth.* 3.

ARISTA'GORAS. Victor, *Nem.* 11.

ARISTOKLEI'DES. Victor, *Nem.* 3.

ARISTO'MENES. Victor, *Pyth.* 8.

ARISTO'TELES. The true (Greek) name of Battos. *Pyth.* 5.

ARKE'SILAS. victor. *Pyth.* 14, 5.

ARSI'NOË. The nurse of Orestes (variously named in other versions of the story). *Pyth.* 11.

ASO'PICHOS. Victor, *Ol.* 14.

ASO'POS. A river (and river-god) in Boiotïa, father of the nymphs Aigina and Thebe. *Isth.* 8.

ASO'POS. A river in Sikyon. *Nem.* 9.

ASTYDAMEI'A. The wife of Tlepolemos. *Ol.* 7.

ATABY'RIOS. A mountain in Rhodes, sacred to Zeus. *Ol.* 7.

ATREI'DAI. Agamemnon and Menelaos, the sons of Atreus. *Isth.* 5.

AU'GEAS. King of the Epeians, whose stables Herakles was forced to clean. *Ol.* 10.

Bas'sidai. The family or clan to which Alkimidas belonged. *Nem.* 6.

Battos. Of Thera, founder and first king of Kyrene. His true name appears to have been Aristoteles, Battos being a nickname or (more probably) a Libyan title. *Pyth.* 4, 5.

Blep'siadai. The family or clan of Alkimedon. *Ol.* 8.

Boi'bias. A lake in Thessaly. *Pyth.* 3.

Bo'reas. The god of the north wind. *Pyth.* 4.

Cha'riadai. The family or clan to which Deinias belonged. *Nem.* 8.

Cha'riklo. Wife of Chiron. *Pyth.* 4.

Chimai'ra. A fabulous beast killed by Bellerophon. *Ol.* 13.

Chiron. The wise and kind centaur, teacher of Jason, Peleus, Asklepios, and other heroes. He was son of Kronos and Philyra, therefore half-brother of Zeus. *Pyth.* 3, 4, 9, etc.

Chro'mios. Victor, *Nem.* 1, 9.

Damai'os. A cult name ("the tamer") of Poseidon. *Ol.* 13.

Da'naos. A legendary Egyptian prince, who fled from his brother Aigyptos to Argos with his fifty daughters. They were pursued there by the fifty sons of Aigyptos, who forced Danaos to give them his daughters in marriage. All the brides except Hypermestra murdered their husbands on their wedding night. *Pyth.* 9, *Nem.* 10.

Darda'nians. Trojans. *Nem.* 3.

Da'rdanos. Son of Zeus, ancestor of the kings of Troy. *Ol.* 13.

Dawn's child. Memnon. *Ol.* 2.

Dei'nias. Victor, *Nem.* 8.

Deino'menes. Father of Hieron. *Pyth.* 1, 2.

Deino'menes. Son of Hieron. *Pyth.* 1.

Delos. The birthplace of Apollo. *Ol.* 6, etc.

Dia'goras. Victor, *Ol.* 7.

Diome'des. A hero prominent in the Trojan War, worshiped in various places in Italy. *Nem.* 10.

Dirke. A river near Thebes. *Ol.* 10, *Isth.* 1, etc.

Di'thyramb. A hymn in honor of Dionysos, one of the elements from which tragedy evolved. *Ol.* 13.

Dodo'na. A place in northwestern Greece, sacred to Zeus. *Nem.* 4.

Dorian, Dorians. A people said to have conquered a large part of southern Greece about two generations after the Trojan War. As the conquerors mixed with the conquered peoples, no Greek states were entirely Dorian; but the Dorian element was predominant in (among other states) Sparta, Argos, Korinth, Aigina, Kyrene. *Ol.* 1, *Pyth.* 1, etc.

Eila'tidas. Aipytos. *Ol.* 6.

Eleithy'ia. The goddess of childbirth. *Ol.* 6, *Nem.* 7, etc.

Elis. The state which, in Pindar's time, controlled Olympia. *Ol.* 1, 9, etc.

Emme'nidai. The family or clan of Theron. *Ol.* 3, *Pyth.* 6.

Enda'is. Wife of Aiakos, mother of Peleus and Telamon. *Nem.* 5.

Enya'lios. Ares. *Ol.* 13, *Isth.* 6.

E'paphos. An Egyptian divinity said by the Greeks to be the son of Io and Zeus, father of Libya. *Pyth.* 4, *Nem.* 10.

163

EPEI'ANS. An ancient name for the people of Elis. *Ol.* 9, 10.

EPHARMOS'TOS. Victor, *Ol.* 9.

EPHYRAI'ANS. Of Ephyra, in Thessaly. The choir who sang *Pythia* 10 were apparently from this place.

EPIAL'TES. *See* OTOS.

ERA'TIDAI. The family or clan of Diagoras. *Ol.* 7.

ERGO'TELES. Victor, *Ol.* 12.

ERIBOI'A. Wife of Telamon. *Isth.* 6.

ERI'NYS, *plural* ERINYES. A Fury, the Furies. *Ol.* 2.

ERIPHY'LE. Wife of Amphiaraos, who was bribed into persuading him to take part in the expedition against Thebes. *Nem.* 9.

ERITI'MOS. A relative of Xenophon. *Ol.* 13.

EUPHRO'SYNA. One of the Graces. *Ol.* 14.

EURI'POS. The strait at Aulis, between Boiotia and Euboia, where Agamemnon's fleet was stormbound and Iphigeneia was sacrificed. *Pyth.* 11.

EURO'TAS. The river on which Sparta is built. *Ol.* 6; *Isth.* 1, 5.

EURY'ALA. One of the Gorgons. *Pyth.* 12.

EURYS'THEUS. King of Argos, to whom Herakles was in bondage and at whose orders he performed the twelve labors. *Ol.* 3, *Pyth.* 9.

EURY'TOS. *See* MOLIONES.

EUTHY'MENES. Uncle of Pytheas and Phylakidas. *Nem.* 5, *Isth.* 6.

EUXINE SEA. The Black Sea. *Nem.* 4.

GE'RYON. A legendary king in the remote west, whose cattle Herakles stole. *Isth.* 1.

GLAUKOS. Grandson of Bellerophon, a Lykian hero who fought on the side of Troy. *Ol.* 13.

HAIMO'NIA. Thessaly. *Nem.* 4.

HARMO'NIA. Wife of Kadmos. *Pyth.* 3, 11.

HE'BE. Goddess of youth, bride of the deified Herakles. *Nem.* 1, 7, etc.

HE'LENOS. Son of Priam. *Nem.* 3.

HE'LIKON. A mountain in Boiotia, home of the Muses. *Isth.* 2.

HE'LIOS. The sun and the sun-god. *Ol.* 7, *Pyth.* 4, *Isth.* 5.

HELO'ROS. A river in Sicily. *Nem.* 9.

HERO'DOTOS. Victor, *Isth.* 1.

HES'TIA. The goddess of the hearth. *Nem.* 11.

HI'ERON. Tyrant of Syracuse; victor, *Ol.* 1; *Pyth.* 1, 2, 3.

HI'MERA. An important city in Sicily. There were famous warm springs there, sacred to the Nymphs. *Ol.* 12.

HIP'PARIS. A river at Kamarina. *Ol.* 5.

HIPPO'KLEAS. Victor, *Pyth.* 10.

HIPPO'LYTA. Wife of Akastos. *Nem.* 4, 5.

HYLLOS. Son of Herakles, ancestor of one of the three Dorian tribes. *Pyth.* 1.

HYPERBORE'ANS. A mythical (or mythically imagined) people who lived "at the back of the north wind." *Ol.* 3, *Pyth.* 10, *Isth.* 5.

HYPERE'IS. A spring at Pherai, near Iolkos. *Pyth.* 4.

HYPERMES'TRA. *See* DANAOS.

HYPSI'PYLE. Queen of the women of Lemnos. *Ol.* 4.

164

IA'LYSOS. Grandson of Helios and Rhodes, after whom one of the Rhodian cities is said to have been named. *Ol.* 7.

IA'PETOS. Grandfather of Deukalion. *Ol.* 9.

IDA. A mountain on Krete, where Zeus was born. *Ol.* 5.

IDAS. Son of Aphareus, the strongest of all men of his time. He was killed by Zeus in the fight with Kastor and Polydeukes. *Nem.* 10.

ILAS. The friend and trainer of Agesidamos. *Ol.* 10.

INO. Daughter of Kadmos, who went mad and killed her own children. She leapt into the sea and became a sea-goddess. *Ol.* 2, *Pyth.* 11.

IOLA'OS. The nephew and comrade-in-arms of Herakles. Games were held in his honor near Thebes. *Ol.* 9, *Isth.* 1, etc.

IOL'KOS. A town in Magnesia. *Pyth.* 4; *Nem.* 3, 4; *Isth.* 8.

IONIAN SEA. The sea west of Greece and south of the Adriatic. *Pyth.* 3.

I'PHIKLES. Brother of Herakles, father of Iolaos. *Pyth.* 9, *Isth.* 1.

IPHI'ON. Presumably the father of Alkimedon. *Ol.* 8.

I'RASA. A city in Libya near Kyrene. *Pyth.* 9.

ISME'NOS. A river at Thebes. *Nem.* 9, 11.

ISTROS. The Danube. *Ol.* 3, 8.

KADMEI'ANS. The inhabitants of Thebes in the heroic age. *Pyth.* 9, etc.

KADMOS. A Phoenician wanderer who became the legendary founder of Thebes. *Ol.* 2, *Pyth.* 3, etc.

KA'ÏKOS. A river in Mysia. *Isth.* 5.

KAL'LIANAX. Ancestor of Diagoras. *Ol.* 7.

KAL'LIAS. An ancestor or relative of Alkimidas. *Nem.* 6.

KALLI'MACHOS. Thought to be the uncle of Alkimedon. *Ol.* 8.

KAMI'ROS. Grandson of Helios and Rhodes, after whom one of the Rhodian cities is said to have been named. *Ol.* 7.

KASTA'LIA. A spring at Delphoi. *Ol.* 7, 9, etc.

KASTOR. *See* TYNDARIDAI.

KE'PHISIS. The daughter of Kephisos. *Pyth.* 12.

KE'PHISOS. A river in Boiotia. *Pyth.* 4, *Ol.* 14.

KILI'KIA. A country on the coast of Asia Minor. *Pyth.* 1.

KI'NYRAS. Legendary king of Kypros. *Pyth.* 2, *Nem.* 8.

KIRRHA. Strictly, a town near Delphoi, of uncertain location and identity and probably to be distinguished from Krisa. Pindar, however, uses both names loosely as synonyms for Delphoi or Pytho. Kirrha: *Pyth.* 3, 7, 8, 10, 11; Krisa: *Pyth.* 5, 6; *Isth.* 2.

KITHAI'RON. A mountain range between Attika and Boiotia, on the northern slopes of which the Battle of Plataia was fought. *Pyth.* 1.

KLEAN'DROS. Victor, *Isth.* 8.

KLEITOR. A city in Arkadia. *Nem.* 10.

KLEO. One of the Muses. *Nem.* 3.

KLEO'NAI. A city in the northern Peloponnese. *Ol.* 10; *Nem.* 4, 10.

KLEO'NYMOS. Ancestor of Melissos. *Isth.* 3, 4.

KLOTHO. One of the Fates. *Ol.* 1, *Isth.* 6.

KLY'MENOS. Father of Erginos, one of the Argonauts, who is mentioned in *Olympia* 4 only as the "son of Klymenos."

KNOSSOS. The chief city of Krete. *Ol.* 12.

KOIRA'NIDAS. "The son of Koiranos," Polyidos, a Korinthian seer. *Ol.* 13.

KOLCHIS. A land at the eastern end of the Black Sea, whence Jason brought home the Golden Fleece. *Pyth.* 4.

KREON'TIDAS. An ancestor or relative of Alkimidas. *Nem.* 6.

KRE'THEUS. Father of Aison, grandfather of Jason. *Pyth.* 4.

KRISA. *See* KIRRHA.

KRO'NION. "The son of Kronos," that is, Zeus. *Pyth.* 1, etc.

KRONOS. The father of Zeus. *Ol.* 1, etc.

KTE'ATOS. *See* MOLIONES.

KYKNOS. Son of Poseidon, killed by Achilles at Troy. *Ol.* 2, *Isth.* 5.

KYKNOS. Son of Ares, a robber killed by Herakles in their second encounter. *Ol.* 10.

KYLLA'NA. A mountain in Arkadia, where Hermes was born. *Ol.* 6.

KYMÊ. Cumae, on the Italian coast north of Naples. *Pyth.* 1.

KYPRIAN, THE. Aphrodite. *Ol.* 1.

KYPRIS. Aphrodite. *Nem.* 8.

LAB'DAKOS. Ancestor of Melissos. *Isth.* 3.

LA'CHESIS. One of the Fates. *Ol.* 7.

LAÏOS. King of Thebes, father of Oidipous. Oidipous killed him without knowing his identity. The story is well known through the play of Sophocles. *Ol.* 2.

LAKEREI'A. A place in Thessaly. *Pyth.* 3.

LAMPRO'MACHOS. A relative of Epharmostos. *Ol.* 9.

LAO'MEDON. King of Troy, killed by Herakles. *Nem.* 3, *Isth.* 6.

LA'PITHAI. A legendary people of Thessaly. *Pyth.* 9.

LATO. Often called Latona, mother of Artemis and Apollo. *Ol.* 3, 8.

LATO'IDAS. "The son of Lato," Apollo. *Pyth.* 3.

LATTER-BORN, THE. The sons of the Seven against Thebes, who took the city. *Pyth.* 8.

LEMNOS. An island in the northern Aegean. *Ol.* 4; *Pyth.* 1, 4.

LERNA. A place near Argos on the sea. *Ol.* 7.

LINDOS. Grandson of Helios and Rhodes, after whom one of the Rhodian cities is said to have been named. *Ol.* 7.

LOKROS. Descendant of Deukalion, king of the Lokrians, adoptive father of the younger Opous. *Ol.* 9.

LO'XIAS. Apollo. *Pyth.* 3, *Isth.* 7.

LYN'KEUS. Son of Aigyptos, husband of Hypermestra. *Nem.* 10.

LYN'KEUS. Son of Aphareus, "the lynx man," with supernaturally keen sight. *Nem.* 10.

MAGNESIA. A region in southeastern Thessaly. *Pyth.* 2, 3, 4; *Nem.* 5.

MAI'NALON or MAI'NALOS. A mountain in Arkadia. *Ol.* 9.

MANTINE'A. An important city in Arkadia. *Ol.* 10.

MEDES. Used loosely by most Greeks to mean Persians and Persian subjects. *Pyth.* 1.

ME'GAKLES. Victor, *Pyth.* 7.

ME'GARA. An important Dorian city near Athens. *Ol.* 7, *Pyth.* 8, *Nem.* 3.

ME'GARA. Wife of Herakles. *Isth.* 4.

166

MEIDY'LIDAI. The family or clan of Aristomenes. *Pyth.* 8.

MELANIP'POS. A Theban hero. *Nem.* 11.

MELEA'GER. Son of Oineus, famous in the story of the Kalydonian Boar; but in Pindar, as in Homer, thought of primarily as the defender of a beleaguered city. *Isth.* 7.

MELE'SIAS. A wrestler and trainer of wrestlers. *Ol.* 8; *Nem.* 4, 6.

MELIA. Mother by Apollo of two sons. *Pyth.* 11.

MELIS'SOS. Victor, *Isth.* 3, 4.

MENAN'DROS. Trainer of Pytheas. *Nem.* 5.

MENOI'TIOS. Son of Aktor and Aigina, father of Patroklos. *Ol.* 9.

ME'ROPES. A legendary people of the island of Kos. *Nem.* 4, *Isth.* 6.

ME'TOPE. A Stymphalian nymph, mother of Thebe. *Ol.* 6.

MIDAS. Victor, *Pyth.* 12.

MI'DEA. The mother of Likymnios. *Ol.* 7.

MI'DEA. A town near Argos. *Ol.* 10.

MI'NYAI. A people of Orchomenos and southern Thessaly; also, a collective name for the Argonauts. *Ol.* 14, *Pyth.* 4.

MOLIO'NES. Eurytos and Kteatos, twin sons of Poseidon and nephews of Augeas. They waylaid and defeated Herakles and his army, but Herakles later ambushed them in turn and killed both. *Ol.* 10.

MOLOS'SIA. A half-Greek kingdom on the Adriatic. *Nem.* 7.

MYR'MIDONS. The legendary subjects of Aiakos and of Achilles. *Nem.* 3.

NE'REUS. A sea-god, father of the Nereids, who were sea-nymphs. *Ol.* 2, *Pyth.* 3, *Nem.* 3, *Isth.* 8.

NIKASIP'POS. Presumably, the trainer of the choir for *Isthmia* 2.

NISOS. A legendary king of Megara. *Pyth.* 9, *Nem.* 5.

O'IKLES. Father of Amphiaraos. *Pyth.* 8, etc.

OI'NEUS. Legendary king of Aitolia. *Isth.* 5.

OINO'NA. The island of Aigina. *Nem.* 4, etc.

OINO'PIA. Oinona. *Isth.* 8.

OLIGAI'THIDAI. The family or clan of Xenophon. *Ol.* 13.

ONCHES'TOS. A place in Boiotia, sacred to Poseidon. *Isth.* 1, 5.

O'POUS. (1) A king of the Epeians in Elis. (2) The son of Opous' daughter and Zeus, adopted by Lokros. The younger Opous is not directly named but is described as being called after his mother's father. *Ol.* 9.

ORESTES. Son of Agamemnon, of Lakonia (Lakedaimon), according to Stesichoros and Pindar; of Mykenai or Argos, according to others. *Pyth.* 11, *Nem.* 11.

OR'SEAS. Trainer of Melissos. *Isth.* 4.

ORTHOSIA. A cult-name of Artemis. *Ol.* 3.

ORTY'GIA. An island, sacred to Artemis, forming part of the city of Syracuse. *Ol.* 6, *Pyth.* 2, *Nem.* 1.

OTOS. A giant, brother of Epialtes. *Pyth.* 4.

PAM'PHAËS. Ancestor of Theaios. *Nem.* 10.

PAM'PHYLOS. Ancestor of one of the Dorian tribes. *Pyth.* 1.

PANGAI'OS *or* PANGAION. A mountain in Thrace. *Pyth.* 4.

PARNAS'SOS. The great mountain above Delphoi, which is built on one of its spurs, overlooking a deep valley. *Ol.* 9; *Pyth.* 1, 10, etc.

PARRHA'SIANS. A people of Arkadia, in charge of the games for Zeus Lykaios. *Ol.* 9.

PEIRA'NA. A spring in Korinth. *Ol.* 13.

PEISAN'DROS. A legendary Spartan colonist of Tenedos, ancestor of Aristagoras. *Nem.* 11.

PELEI'ADAS. The son of Peleus, Achilles. *Pyth.* 6.

PELEI'ADES. The Pleiades; in Greek legend the daughters of Atlas. *Nem.* 2.

PELIN'NA. A place in Thessaly on the Peneios, home of Hippokleas. *Pyth.* 10.

PE'LION. A wooded mountain in Magnesia, the home of the centaurs. *Pyth.* 2, 3, etc.

PELOPS. Son of Tantalos, grandfather of Agamemnon and Menelaos. The southern peninsula of Greece, the Peloponnese ("island of Pelops"), was supposed to have been named after him. *Ol.* 1, 3, etc.

PENEI'OS. A large river in Thessaly, and its river-god. *Pyth.* 9, 10.

PER'GAMON *or* PERGAMOS. Troy. *Ol.* 8.

PERIKLY'MENOS. The Theban champion who put Amphiaraos to flight. *Nem.* 9.

PHAISA'NA. An Arkadian or Elian town of uncertain location. *Ol.* 6.

PHA'LARIS. Tyrant of Akragas in the early sixth century B.C. *Pyth.* 1.

PHASIS. A river in Kolchis. *Pyth.* 4, *Isth.* 2.

PHERENI'KOS. A race horse belonging to Hieron. *Ol.* 1, *Pyth.* 3.

PHILOKTE'TES. Son of Poias, an Achaian hero, who inherited the bow of Herakles. Infected by a snake bite on his way to Troy with Agamemnon, he was marooned on Lemnos; but since it was fated that Troy could be captured only with the aid of Herakles' bow, the Achaians were forced to send an embassy and persuade him to return. The story is told by many ancient authors, with many variants. *Pyth.* 1.

PHI'LYRA. The mother of Chiron. *Pyth.* 3, 4, etc.

PHINTIS. Presumably the charioteer of Agesias. *Ol.* 6.

PHLEGRAI'AN FIELDS. A volcanic region near Naples. *Nem.* 1, *Isth.* 6.

PHLE'GYAS. The father of Koronis. *Pyth.* 3.

PHOKOS. Son of Aiakos and Psamatheia, half-brother of Peleus and Telamon. He was murdered by them, and this was why these heroes were forced to leave Aigina. *Nem.* 5.

PHORKOS. Father of the Graiai, the three aged women whose one eye was stolen by Perseus. *Pyth.* 12.

PHRIXOS. Son of Athamas. He escaped from the attacks of his stepmother, Ino, by means of the golden-fleeced ram, which carried him to Kolchis. There Phrixos sacrificed the ram and hung up the fleece. The story is told with many variants. Phrixos was a cousin of Jason and Pelias. *Pyth.* 4.

PHTHIA. A part of Thessaly, the home of Achilles. *Pyth.* 3, *Nem.* 4.

PHYLA'KA. A city in Thessaly. *Isth.* 1.

PHYLA'KIDAS. Victor, *Isth.* 5, 6.

PIE'RIDES. The Muses, of Pieria. *Ol.* 10, *Pyth.* 1, etc.

PINDOS. A mountain range in north-central Greece, once the home of the Dorians. *Pyth.* 1, 9.

POLYDEU'KES. *See* TYNDARIDAI.

168

POLYMNA'STOS. The father of Battos. *Pyth.* 4.

POLYNEI'KES. Son of Oidipous. He and his brother, Eteokles, were to rule Thebes in turn after Oidipous was driven out. Eteokles broke the agreement. Polyneikes fled to Argos, married the daughter of Adrastos, and returned with the Seven against Thebes to attack his own city. Polyneikes and Eteokles killed each other. The attack on the city was repulsed, but the sons of the Seven Champions took Thebes in the next generation. (Cf. Aeschylus, *The Seven against Thebes;* Sophocles, *Antigone, Oidipous at Kolonos;* Euripides, *The Phoenician Women.*) *Ol.* 2.

POLYTI'MIDAS. A brother (probably) of Alkimidas. *Nem.* 6.

PROITOS. Legendary king of Tiryns. *Nem.* 10.

PROTESILA'OS. A Thessalian hero, killed at Troy. *Isth.* 1.

PROTOGENEI'A. Daughter of Deukalion and Pyrrha. *Ol.* 9.

PSAMATHEI'A. "The girl of the sand," mother of Phokos by Aiakos. *Nem.* 5.

PSAUMIS. Victor, *Ol.* 4, 5.

PTOIODO'ROS. A relative of Xenophon. *Ol.* 13.

PY'LADES. Comrade-in-arms of Orestes. *Pyth.* 11.

PY'THEAS. Victor, *Nem.* 5.

RHADAMAN'THYS. One of the judges of the dead. *Ol.* 2, *Pyth.* 2.

RHEA. Mother of Zeus. *Ol.* 2, *Nem.* 11.

SALMO'NEUS. Father of Tyro, grandfather of Pelias, who attempted to assume the thunderbolt of Zeus and was struck down. *Pyth.* 4.

SE'MELE. Daughter of Kadmos and mother, by Zeus, of Dionysos. *Ol.* 2, *Pyth.* 11.

SE'RIPHOS. An island in the Aegean, where Danae and Perseus were washed ashore. When Perseus returned with the Gorgon's head, the wicked king, Polydektes, and his people were turned to stone. *Pyth.* 12.

SI'KYON. A Dorian city on the Gulf of Korinth. *Ol.* 13, etc.

SI'PYLOS. A mountain in Lydia. *Ol.* 1.

SI'SYPHOS. A legendary hero of Korinth, usually described as clever but unscrupulous. *Ol.* 13.

SKYROS. An island in the northwestern Aegean, where Neoptolemos was born. *Nem.* 7.

SO'GENES. Victor, *Nem.* 7.

SO'LYMOI. A barbarous people of Asia Minor. *Ol.* 13.

SO'STRATOS. The father of Agesias. *Ol.* 6.

SOWN MEN. The warriors who sprang up from the ground when Kadmos sowed the dragon's teeth, that is, the Kadmeians of legend. *Isth.* 7.

STREPSI'ADES. Victor, *Isth.* 7.

STRO'PHIOS. Legendary king of Phokis, father of Pylades. *Pyth.* 11.

STYM'PHALOS. A town in Arkadia. *Ol.* 6.

TAI'NARON. A mountainous promontory of the southern Peloponnese, often spoken of as an entrance to Hades. *Pyth.* 4.

TA'LAOS. Father of Adrastos. *Nem.* 9.

TAY'GETA. A Lakedaimonian nymph, sacred to Artemis. *Ol.* 3.

TAŸ'GETOS. A mountain range overlooking the valley of Sparta. *Pyth.* 1, *Nem.* 10.

TE'GEA. An important city in Arkadia. *Ol.* 10, *Nem.* 10.

TEIRE'SIAS. A legendary seer of Thebes, prominent in Sophoclean tragedy. *Nem.* 1, *Isth.* 7.

TE'LEPHOS. A Mysian hero. When the Achaians invaded his land, on the way to Troy, he put them all to flight until wounded by Achilles. *Ol.* 9; *Isth.* 5, 8.

TELESI'KRATES. Victor, *Pyth.* 9.

TERP'SIAS. A relative of Xenophon. *Ol.* 13.

TEUKROS. Son of Telamon, half-brother of Aias. *Nem.* 4.

TEUTHRAS. King of Mysia in Asia Minor. *Ol.* 9.

THA'LIA. One of the Graces. *Ol.* 14.

THEAI'OS. Victor, *Nem.* 10.

THEAN'DRIDAI. The family or clan of Timasarchos. *Nem.* 4.

THEA'RION. The building allotted to the *theoroi,* who were designated to consult oracles on behalf of the state. *Nem.* 3.

THE'BE. The nymph of Thebes, daughter of Asopos and Metope, sister of Aigina. *Ol.* 6, etc.

THEMIS. Goddess of order. *Ol.* 8, etc.

THEMIS'TIOS. Grandfather of Pytheas and Phylakidas. *Nem.* 5, *Isth.* 6.

THERA. A Dorian island in the southern Aegean. *Pyth.* 4, 5.

THERAP'NE. A place near Sparta. *Pyth.* 11, *Nem.* 10, *Isth.* 1.

THERON. Tyrant of Akragas, victor, *Ol.* 2, 3.

THERSAN'DROS. Son of Polyneikes, ancestor of Theron. *Ol.* 2.

THORAX. Lord of Larisa, patron (perhaps an elder relative?) of Hippokleas. *Pyth.* 10.

THRASYBOU'LOS. Son of Xenokrates, nephew of Theron. *Pyth.* 6, *Isth.* 2.

THRASYDAI'OS. Victor, *Pyth.* 11.

THYO'NA. Semele. *Pyth.* 3.

TIMASAR'CHOS. Victor, *Nem.* 4.

TIMODA'MOS. Victor, *Nem.* 2.

TIMO'STHENES. Brother of Alkimedon. *Ol.* 8.

TI'RYNS. A city near Argos. *Ol.* 7, 10; *Isth.* 6.

TI'TYOS. Son of Zeus, king of Panopeus, killed by Artemis for trying to attack Lato. *Pyth.* 4.

TYNDA'RIDAI. The "sons of Tyndareus," Kastor and Polydeukes (Pollux). *Ol.* 3, etc.

TYRO. Mother, by Poseidon, of Pelias. *Pyth.* 4.

TYRSE'NIAN. Etruscan. *Pyth.* 1.

XENO'KRATES. Brother of Theron, victor, *Pyth.* 6.

XE'NOPHON. Victor, *Ol.* 13.

PHOENIX BOOKS
in Art, Music, Poetry, and Drama